Wounded to Warrior Woman

through Faith, Family, Fitness, Food and Fun

Kristen Nugent, Ph.D.

Printed in the United States of America

First Printing, 2019

ISBN 978-1-7330140-1-4

Scripture quotations taken from the New American Standard Bible® (NASB), Copyright © 1960, 1962, 1963, 1968, 1971, 1972, 1973, 1975, 1977, 1995 by The Lockman Foundation. Used by permission. www.Lockman.org

The information provided in this book is intended to provide helpful information on the subjects discussed. This book is not meant to be used, nor should it be used, to diagnose or treat any medical or mental condition. For diagnosis or treatment of any such problem, readers should consult his or her own qualified professional. The publisher and author are not liable for any damages or negative consequences from any treatment, action, application or preparation, to any person reading or following the information in this book. References do not in every case constitute endorsement of any websites or other sources.

Logo design by Mark Nugent

FAITH FAMILY FITNESS and FUN

Table of Contents

For my dragons

Will, I love how God made us the mother/son team. You are amazing!

Lily, I love how God made you "the chosen one."

You are a joy machine!

Mark, I love how God made you – full of integrity, playful,

and truly delightful!

Thank you to Emma, Kay, Laura, Madison, and Michelle,

for adding their voices to the story.

Special thanks to Lana Wildman who challenges me to use my voice
and step forward with courage. This book would not have been
written if it wasn't for you, Lana. Thank you for walking with me and
for all of your help to make this book happen!

In loving memory of Fran McAleavey

Introduction

This book is for the weary woman trying to hold it together, hiding pain and brokenness, wondering if this is all there is. This is for those precious, wounded women who are trying to be strong, moms, students, wives, businesswomen, trying to minister to their families and communities and co-workers and wondering where they're going to find the strength for tomorrow.

There are a lot of self-care books on the shelves for the walking wounded. The wisdom that the offer is practical, but, in my opinion, they do not go far enough. I want to examine Faith, Family, Fitness, Food and Fun in the light of a relationship with Jesus Christ. As our prime example, Jesus Christ has a lot to say about how we live our lives in the midst of our current situations.

We need to consult the manual He wrote regarding the bodies and the nature He created us with and find the best practices we can. Self-care without a lens of Christian spirituality might be somewhat effective. However, I believe that looking at the same personal disciplines in the light of Scripture provides a more compelling case for self-care and sets us more in line with God's original intention for an abundant, victorious life.

This is not just another bunch of preaching with no personal application behind it. I'm bringing you these ideas from my own struggles with addiction, being overweight, growing up in a dysfunctional family, and doing all the right things for all the wrong reasons but not getting anywhere. I may have some education, but I promise you I've learned far more in the trenches with God than all my degrees could have taught me.

Faith, Family, Fitness, Food and Fun might not be the only areas you can focus on for practical and effective self-care, but they are five of the most significant, because they comprise the largest portions of our daily living. I want to show you how a personal repertoire of regular practices in each of these areas can do amazing things to lessen the amount of stress you carry around. You can also experience victory in those very issues you've struggled with for so long.

If the loudest voice in your quiet moments whispers in your heart that you're a mess, that you'll never lead a fulfilled and abundant life, that God doesn't care about you and that you certainly don't deserve better than what you've got now, this is the book for you. Don't lose any more of your life to the lies. I will show you what change looked like for me.

Open your battered heart one more time, promise yourself you'll be courageous, and take a deep breath. I have some good news, and that is that you can have an abundant life and you can be a warrior woman!

1 - A Hot Mess Looking Good

Can you relate to any of these women?

- The girl struggling with a speech impediment and learning disability at school, with neither classmates nor teachers willing to help her
- A single mom trying to raise a son who would not succumb to the statistics that haunt young men without a father figure in the house
- The family trying to figure out how to survive on the loss of an income for the family when there are special medical needs looming
- A woman looking to her church group for support during a time of great emotional, spiritual, and ministry need—and finding none
- The woman who has dealt with being overweight for most of her life, finally realizing that she is out of her depth in a controlling addiction
- The couple trying to get pregnant, to no avail
- The survivor of a dysfunctional family trying to learn the dynamics of a healthy relationship in her second marriage

All those people I described are the same person.

I know, you're thinking "What a mess!" and maybe even "Wow, I'm glad I'm not her!"
You know something?

That person was me!

From the age of nine, I coped with overweight, learning disabilities, and rejection by those around me. Life went from crisis to crisis while I struggled along under lifelong issues that compounded one another and stacked up. Over the years, I learned a lot of coping mechanisms that generally led to other problems instead of helping with anything at all. I was the poster child for the term "walking wounded."

Nobody knew, because I could fake it really well. For everyone else, I was the problem solver and the strong one. Some of my more perceptive friends might have sensed that I was stressing over something, but no one ever got all the gory details of my hurt and frustration and anger and lostness and defeat. Deep down, I believed that I was the problem and that I didn't matter.

It all came to the tipping point while my husband and I were trying to cope with the stress of our international adoption. I finally realized that I was done. I had no more emotional, spiritual, mental, or physical energy wherewith to function well any more. And I couldn't fake it any more.

I was wounded, and finally, I was in BURNOUT.

Burnout
Per Merriam-Webster, the definition of *burnout* is

1: the cessation of operation usually of a jet or rocket engine; *also*: the point at which burnout occurs
2: exhaustion of physical or emotional strength or motivation usually as a result of prolonged stress or frustration (Merriam-Webster.com)

Put a little more eloquently by the Urban Dictionary online, burnout is "a state of emotional and physical exhaustion caused by a prolonged period of stress and frustration; an inevitable corporate condition characterized by frequent displays of unprofessional behavior, a blithe refusal to do any work, and most important, a distinct aura of not giving a [term not fit for polite company]."

Yes, my powerful, multi-tasking woman's rocket engine had finally fizzled out.

***

I love being a university professor.

It is truly an honor to help students get ready for entering their chosen helping profession. As a degree requirement at my university, students are required to complete a field placement of a certain number of hours within their area of study. Part of their field placement experience includes a weekly seminar, which is a place and time for students to bring up their concerns related to field placement. Over and over, my astounded students tell me stories of the tough situations they and their colleagues find themselves in. Or they tell me their own stories of personal struggles they are coping with while they are in school and beginning their career.

I also work with clients in private practice. When I completed my Ph.D. and began private practice, I was distressed to see, that first year, that most of my clients were highly qualified Bachelor's and Master's degree practitioners in the helping professions. I still see this, women and men who are suffering from physical, mental, and emotional issues at the same time they are coping with incredibly demanding careers. These dear people possess huge hearts and yearn to change the world, but they are barely surviving life. Some are even Christians in all kinds of ministry, but they have no experience of the abundant life Christ came to establish.

One of the things I hear over and over through the years is some exhausted variation of "It isn't working any more. I don't know what to do." In many cases, they already had mentally checked out and were staying for the paycheck.

But that isn't just in my world with helping professionals. I see the same expressions on the faces of people everywhere.

A frazzled-looking mom tugging a whining three-year-old through the grocery while trying to placate a screaming infant strapped into a carrier.

A cashier in tears, trying to smile and be polite after being reamed out by a livid customer for something that wasn't her fault that she couldn't fix.

An overweight young woman sitting on the walking track at the gym, beet red, perspiring and weeping because she doesn't have the energy to complete one circuit.

I see a lot of wounded, burned out women.

I see YOU.

Are you wounded and burned out, dear one? Are you weary and frustrated with life and not sure why you keep trying? Why did you pick up this book? Something about the title and the back copy caught your interest.

Take a look below. Can you relate to any of this?

> **Mental**
> Can't stop thinking about problems
> Forgetfulness, difficulty concentrating
> Difficulty making choices
> Diminished productivity
> Indifference or resentment for necessary activities, whether at home or work
> Loss of coping skills

Physical
Poor eating
Poor sleep or insomnia
Frequent or persistent illness
Fatigue and low energy

Emotional
Anger, irritation, impatience, resentment
Numbness or apathy toward others
Fear, worry and anxiety
Increased pessimism, sense of hopelessness, generally
negative attitude
Depression
Thoughts of suicide or self-harm

Behavioral
Addiction to drugs or alcohol or food
Increased use of distraction behaviors (gambling shopping,
pornography)
Estrangement or isolation from friends/ family
Engaging in risky or reckless activities

Spiritual
No prayer life
No personal Bible study
Low or no church attendance
No habit of personal devotions
No attitude of gratitude

Overall
NO JOY IN LIFE!

Look back over that list. Which of those did you mentally mark?
Honestly, you precious lady. One per grouping? Two per grouping?
More?
Has your powerful woman's rocket engine fizzled?

I'm glad you picked up this book, because I want to share some of the
best ideas I know for getting to a place of joy and conviction that life is

very good! These bits of wisdom are what changed me from wounded to warrior woman, and I know they'll work for you.

The thief comes only to steal and kill and destroy; I came that they may have life, and have it abundantly. John 10:10

A warrior woman's abundant life

Imagine waking every day with the certainty that you are doing what you're supposed to be doing, in the right place, doing the tasks God designed for you to do. Imagine that you can feel God's closeness all around while you're moving through your day, whether you're tending to little ones or performing a ballet or giving PowerPoint presentations to hundreds of people.

Wouldn't that bring new energy to your whole life? To your work and your efforts? God intends for us to walk that intimately with Him. Everything He does and everything He allows to come into our lives is meant to draw us closer to Him in more and more dependence. And when we are so close to God, we hear and follow those promptings of the Holy Spirit. We do this thing, we speak to that person, we keep working at this certain project, and we can see the Kingdom of God being built right before us. And that is our calling as Christians.

Our faith in and relationship with God should be the first and foremost difference-makers in our lives. Because we know God's love for us and Christ's sacrifice on our behalf, we understand the value of what we are doing and the worth of those we are serving, be they family, co-workers, or strangers we meet. When things go sideways and get stressful, we can keep from getting swallowed up by the darkness because of His presence with us every moment and the hope we have for eternity with Him.

If we are in right relationship with God, then we possess all that we need to live well and minister well in His name. That's the kind of radical view you won't find in most of those books about recovering from and avoiding burnout. While they have some good and practical ideas, the end is to serve and please yourself. But you and I know that serving and pleasing ourselves is not what it's all about.

God shows up

I want to make it clear that it is God who will show you the way when it comes to recovering from burnout, but we—you and I—must do the hard work of applying the wisdom to our lives.

Because He sees our situations very clearly, He can lead us into the healing and wisdom we are longing for. He will direct our minds and hearts to His Word and His will. He will lead us to new understandings in both in specific situations and for daily living in general. Because He knows our needs much better than we know them ourselves, He is infinitely more qualified to show us the way through and out of our pain and stuckness.

I will instruct you and teach you in the way which you should go; I will counsel you with My eye upon you. Psalm 32:8.

However, we must cooperate with Him by making room in our lives for Him to work. I am talking about learning to soften our hearts that may be so hard against all the hurt and brokenness, making space to invite and experience the peace and love of our Savior as He works to shape us into His likeness and direct our paths where He desires.

Do not be as the horse or as the mule which have no understanding, whose trappings include bit and bridle to hold them in check, otherwise they will not come near to you. Psalm 32:9

It is easy to be reluctant to let God have His way when we think about the size of the darkness we face. We may fear what He may ask of us. But we have two options. First, we can continue to try to convince ourselves that we can do the work on our own, as we see fit. Or we can make the whole process much easier by being open to change, to trying new things, to making self-care with God our new priority.

When life hits like a freight train and all of a sudden we have to admit that we can't hold it together any more, God is there. In our deepest fatigue, sometimes all we can muster up is a teeth-clenching intention to obey when we feel God's leading, even if we don't have any understanding of how or why. We can change our behavior to what we know is right, and then we sit quietly with our hearts and minds as open as we possibly can, expecting God to bring understanding and healing. And God will show up! He won't force us to receive from Him. When we insist on fussing and try to tweak it our own way, He'll stay out of the way and let us struggle. But when we offer God an expectant, conditions-free heart, He will show up!

But I'm a Christian!

I rejoice if you call Jesus Christ your Savior and Lord and are committed to walking with Him. You are in the best position to get the answers you need. However, I've been around the block a few times, and I've figured out that sometimes the ideas that seem like they should be answers actually turn out to add to the problem.

I've talked to many Christians who have convinced themselves that because they're Christians, they are immune—or they should be—to the pressures under which other people fall. They have expectations that they should be "all things to all people" and "do all things through Christ who strengthens" them. Therefore, if they are not serving tirelessly and perfectly, they are sinful and failures.

I thought this way once.

I've talked to Christians who believe that self-care is for selfish people and that it's wrong to be so selfish.

As a Christian, before I really discovered the amazing grace of a relationship with Jesus Christ, I thought this, too.

My heart breaks for these folks, because they are caught in lies that the devil wants them to believe, so he can keep their lives from being full and effective. Christian or not, you're human, and that means that you don't have all the answers right now and you're just as susceptible to weakness and mistakes as the next person. The truth is that you're NOT a failure for not being able to help everybody you want to help, NOT sinful for wanting just one day of your life to go without a problem, NOT selfish for staying in bed when you're sick. Your human frailty does not surprise or disappoint God, but the devil gets a lot of traction by telling struggling Christians otherwise.

8

Let me ask you: how can you be doing all things through Christ who strengthens you if you aren't even availing yourself of ALL that He has to offer you?!

I don't have time!

I find it fascinating when people tell me they don't have time. We live in such a fast-paced society—there is always some way to rationalize not having time for God.

- I am too busy. I'm in school full-time, work full-time and have a full-time family.
- I am busy with young kids.
- I am a single parent with a demanding job.
- I am being pulled in so many directions I'm too tired to take the time when I get a minute to myself.
- I just don't feel like it. It's so hard to get motivated about making the effort.
- I'm okay. I'm doing fine. Things could be a lot worse. I can handle this.

And the list continues.

No time? No need? For God? As Christians? I don't understand this. I can no longer function without God central in my day. The more stress I have in my life, the more of God and the less of myself I need.

Spend a few minutes imagining your life without the level of stress you're dealing with day in and day out. Remember thinking about waking up every day and knowing you were doing exactly what you were meant to do. Remember the peace you felt because God was with you every moment?

The things I'll share in the following pages do take some deliberate time thinking about, praying about, and applying to your everyday life. But I promise you'll find that after a while, you'll discover that it's not time wasted, not time that would have been better spent other ways. After a while, you'll find that the time you spend on these new habits

9

will have changed your life and your outlook on life. I'll even bet that you'll realize that some of your stressors are completely gone.

Being a Christian—in relationship with Jesus Christ—has nothing to do with whether you'll end up facing difficult times. Being a Christian isn't a magical pass to a problem-free life. But knowing God and being close to Him does mean that you have access to the most important tools you can have in recovering from burnout and living a warrior woman's abundant life.

How to use this book

The next chapters will address each of the five F's: Faith, Family, Fitness, Food, and Fun. We'll take a look at each of them in relation to self-care, and see what the Christian Bible has to say about each subject. I want to give you ideas for lifestyle habits you can incorporate into your everyday life. These practices will help you find a way to move away from a state of burnout and also build a strong foundation for going forward, so the hard times that keep coming do not take such a toll on you.

Journal

Each chapter will have lots of questions to ask yourself and journal about. Look for this journal alert. It's your cue to think and write down your honest responses to what I'm saying. If you're reading on an electronic platform, keep a notebook and pen handy for taking notes and writing down your thoughts. If you've got a paper-and-ink book, I hope you'll feel free to underline, highlight, and write right on the pages. Make this your logbook for a great adventure.

Reminder

There are a few reminders scattered here and there, and you can put these into your own words and tape them to your bathroom mirror. They apply to just about everything you're trying to master in your recovery and new approach to life.

Action

All of that said, it's easier to read a book and write down some thoughts compared to actually applying your discoveries into your own personal life. So I'll have a place in each chapter for you to record things you want to try around each topic, right next to a place to record the dates you commit to accomplish each new challenge. This book is about taking action.

Prayer

I've included some examples of prayers for you to make your own or change to express your own heart. Prayer—talking to God—will be a precious activity all throughout this book.

Check In

Each chapter will end with a Check In. These little assessments aren't going to be graded—no one else has to see them—but I do want you to take the time to answer them honestly. Get a clear picture of where you are in terms of how you handle stress. Put some concrete responses to things you might not have admitted to anyone else, possibly even to yourself.

Things may get uncomfortable for a while as you do some soul searching and try new things. But, I promise, they won't stay uncomfortable. The work you're about to do now will serve to set you up for the abundant life God designed you to live!

You are not alone in your woundedness and burnout. I've been where you are and I remember how hard it can be. I also know how good it is when you look back one day and realize how much hard work you've really done. Dear woman, there is nothing more important than your freedom and safety in Jesus Christ, and I've done my best to show you a clear path.

Most importantly—and I cannot express how much I hope you know this—God is with you. The same God who created the stars, sky, and moon. The same God who healed the sick and brought Jesus back from death to life. He is with you to help you and He is far more interested in your journey than you are. Do you believe that God has all power? Do you believe that He cares about you?

But from there you will seek the Lord your God, and you will find Him if you search for Him with all your heart and all your soul. Deuteronomy 4:29

'For I know the plans that I have for you,' declares the Lord, 'plans for welfare and not for calamity to give you a future and a hope. Then you will call upon Me and come and pray to Me, and I will listen to you. You will seek Me and find Me when you search for Me with all your heart. I will be found by you,' declares the Lord. Jeremiah 29:11-14

2 - FAITH: Doing It God's Way

I embarked upon my career as a medical social worker in a med/surg and toxicology unit at a prominent Pittsburgh hospital. In that situation, I coped with the emotional stress by overeating. By the time I completed my master's degree and returned to the medical setting, I still did not have any kind of support to encourage or force me to develop self-care in terms of setting personal and professional boundaries. I pretty much functioned at a crisis level, moving from problem to problem.

Now I had come to Jesus and been baptized 17 years earlier. I was familiar with the basics of Christianity, but only in my head and outward "Christian" actions, but not my heart. I was saved, but I had no concept of a personal relationship with Jesus Christ. I did not turn to Him for help with my problems: not the little ones I wanted to fix and certainly not the huge issues overshadowing my whole life that I could not even identify. My self-esteem rose and fell on my status and performance in every aspect of my life, to the point that I felt it necessary to obtain a Ph.D. in order to compensate for my inadequacies.

When I went into private practice, I over-functioned for my clients, taking all kinds of responsibility upon myself without putting any responsibility back on them. For example, sometimes I didn't charge for services. I overscheduled clients or I accepted clients who were not receptive to help. While playing the savior to them, I did not recognize that I needed a savior myself. I didn't realize that I didn't have all the answers like I thought I did (or should!).

I did finally realize it. This point came when I was a regular church-goer, heavily involved in the women's Bible study (and also acting as a fixer for people—Kris has lots of resources and she loves to help people, so call Kris!) However, this all came to a screeching halt when I at last reached out to my church and Bible study friends. My husband and I had decided to adopt a 3-year-old girl from China, and I expected people from church would want to walk alongside us in such a momentous undertaking. It was a big thing and I wanted a support system of like-minded people on a regular basis.

It rocked me when there was no support. Not even when I directly asked. "I can't do anything to help you," they said, or "I didn't know you needed help."

There was not even a follow-up contact from the Bible study when I stopped attending due to the demands of my new daughter's medical diagnoses.

We stopped attending that church, and I had a huge lightbulb moment when, from that whole group of women into whom I had poured so much for three years, there was not one phone call to find out where I'd gone. I'd thought they were good friends, but when I was desperate and asking for help for the first time, all those relationships were a puff of smoke.

And I realized I was the problem. From all my woundedness, I'd learned to isolate myself and from that dark place, I'd tried every kind of solution under the sun, from Buddhism to therapy, everything but God. But because I didn't know how relationships were supposed to work, I didn't know how to connect to people. I was too immature to understand what true friendship meant, and I'd spent all that time connecting with people who had only shown me what I had shown them.

14

Long story short, I had functioned a long time looking good and doing good and convincing myself that I was doing well. But when one final crisis tipped me over the edge, I realized nothing I was building my life on could support the important things. I admitted that I was wounded to the core and didn't know how to stop the bleeding.

There was nothing else I could do—I was forced to trust God and open my heart to Him. It was baby steps all along the way, opening my heart to God, learning to trust Him, letting His love and light in.

That was the self-care that was going to work an amazing change in my life!

The practices of faith

Christian faith is belief or trust in God, and spirituality is living out the values of said faith. Together, faith and spirituality give individuals a sense of belonging and purpose, a connection with something larger than themselves. Faith and spirituality also bring people into contact with like-minded others, so there is mutual support around the common purpose.

I found a literature review of 444 studies[1] which looked at the intersection of depression and religious/spiritual practices. Over 60% of the studies reported fewer depressive episodes and quicker recovery from depression in those who practiced religion or spirituality. However, we should not need scientists to tell us that the practices of Christianity are the best tools we have to cope with stress. I will state it unequivocally, and I challenge you to find out for yourself.

Journal

I've dropped the first F on you – Faith. What are you thinking now? Take a minute to write down what you expect from the Faith chapter of the book. Then keep reading.

So what are the practices of Christian faith? Let's start with prayer, engagement with the Bible, a mindset of thanksgiving and praise, fellowship with the body of Christ, and trusting God. How can you put these practices to work? Let's look at the ones that can be considered most important.

Prayer

The Bible speaks clearly about the place prayer should have in our lives.

First of all, then, I urge that entreaties and prayers, petitions and thanksgivings, be made on behalf of all men, for kings and all who are in authority, so that we may lead a tranquil and quiet life in all godliness and dignity. This is good and acceptable in the sight of God our Savior, who desires all men to be saved and to come to the knowledge of the truth. 1 Timothy 2:1-4

Pray about things going on in your life. And while there may be rules about talking to your clients about your beliefs, there's nothing that says you can't pray for them and their situations.

You don't have to know what to pray. God knows what the situation needs. Your prayer can consist of simply bringing it to Him with a request for His help. Try not to pin your hopes and expectations to one certain outcome, because God may have something different in mind.

In the same way the Spirit also helps our weakness; for we do not know how to pray as we should, but the Spirit Himself intercedes for us with groanings too deep for words. Romans 8:26

Prayer is the antidote to worry, the Apostle Paul says. *Be anxious for nothing, but in everything by prayer and supplication with thanksgiving let your requests be made known to God. And the peace of God, which surpasses all comprehension, will guard your hearts and your minds in Christ Jesus.* Philippians 4:6-7

Therefore let us draw near with confidence to the throne of grace, so that we may receive mercy and find grace to help in time of need. Hebrews 4:16

Don't let the idea of prayer be a big scary thing for you. Simply talk to God. Tell Him what you think and feel, tell Him what you need and want. And listen. He may not speak audibly at that moment, but spend some time in an attitude of listening. God will speak to your heart at the right time and you'll begin to recognize His voice and the way He speaks to you. Then, communicating with God will become precious!

Experiment with different ways of praying. It's not just on your knees by your bed. There are lots of things to try—just look online for "ways to pray" or "types of prayer." The point is that you spend time focused on God and listen for Him and set yourself to obey what He may tell you.

Read, memorize, meditate on God's Word.
Your word is a lamp to my feet and a light to my path. Psalm 119:105

Your word I have treasured in my heart, that I may not sin against You. Psalm 119:11

The Bible is full of precious promises for those who do love, trust, and obey Him. God will hear us and send His Holy Spirit to lead us and lift us up!

The Lord will make you the head and not the tail, and you only will be above, and you will not be underneath, if you listen to the commandments of the Lord your God, which I charge you today, to observe them carefully. Deuteronomy 28:13

And we are witnesses of these things; and so is the Holy Spirit, whom God has given to those who obey Him. Acts 5:23

Get in the habit of reading your Bible every day. You can find a through-the-Bible-in-a-year plan and have an amazing journey through God's history with us. Join a Bible study at your church, or begin one on your own by going to a Christian bookstore and finding a Bible study on a topic you find interesting. Don't forget that you can also listen to the Bible—many translations are available on CD or mp3.

Memorize passages which are particularly meaningful to you so you have them with you all day long. Meditation is simply repeating and thinking over one small verse or phrase over and over, letting it speak to you and shape your responses to things coming your way.

Self-respect is the fruit of discipline; the sense of dignity grows with the ability to say no to oneself.
~Abraham Joshua Heschel

Thanksgiving and praise
In everything give thanks; for this is God's will for you in Christ Jesus.
1 Thessalonians 5:18

That's pretty point-blank, isn't it? For good reason. The more you focus on the good and practice gratitude, the easier life becomes.

Rejoice in the Lord always; again I will say, rejoice! Let your gentle spirit be known to all men. The Lord is near. Be anxious for nothing, but in everything by prayer and supplication with thanksgiving let your requests be made known to God. And the peace of God, which surpasses all comprehension, will guard your hearts and your minds in Christ Jesus. Finally, brethren, whatever is true, whatever is honorable, whatever is right, whatever is pure, whatever is lovely, whatever is of good repute, if there is any excellence and if anything worthy of praise, dwell on these things. The things you have learned and received and heard and seen in me, practice these things, and the God of peace will be with you. Philippians 4:4-8
Read that again. Did you catch it? Rejoice. Don't be anxious. Pray about it. Think about the positive. And the God of peace will be with you! A negative outlook just adds to your stress! I promise this is true, not just sappy platitudes babbled off by people with no problems. A little persistent effort in this direction can lead to a big difference in your outlook on life.

Church attendance

How does meeting regularly with fellow believers help us?

And let us consider how to stimulate one another to love and good deeds, not forsaking our own assembling together, as is the habit of some, but encouraging one another; and all the more as you see the day drawing near. Hebrews 10:24-25

We are called to pray for one another, encourage one another, and help each other, but we can do that only if we know what's going on in the lives of those around us.

Bear one another's burdens, and thereby fulfill the law of Christ. Galatians 6:2

Church is another place to hear the Word of God preached and be challenged by it.

Until I come, give attention to the public reading of Scripture, to exhortation and teaching. 1 Timothy 4:13

Consider setting aside one day a week to rest physically and mentally, taking a break from the daily grind to focus on your relationship with God. You may find it hard to think about losing the time you could spend catching up on other things. But you might also find God can make your efforts the rest of the week doubly effective in return for this investment of time with Him.

"If because of the Sabbath, you turn your foot from doing your own pleasure on My holy day, and call the Sabbath a delight, the holy day of the Lord honorable, and honor it, desisting from your own ways, from seeking your own pleasure and speaking your own word, then you will take delight in the Lord, and I will make you ride on the heights of the earth; and I will feed you with the heritage of Jacob your father, for the mouth of the Lord has spoken." Isaiah 58 13-14

Trust and obey

Trust in the Lord with all your heart and do not lean on your own understanding. In all your ways acknowledge Him, and He will make your paths straight. Do not be wise in your own eyes. Fear the Lord and turn away from evil. Proverbs 3: 5-7

What does trusting God look like?

Trusting God is believing and acting in accordance with what God says.

What He says about you, about Himself, about the world.

What He says about sin and about what He did about sin.

What He wants you to do in general, which you know from reading the Bible, and in specific situations, which you know from praying about things and seeking wise Christian counsel.

- Do you trust God to take care of your interests instead of defending your reputation?
- Do you seek God to help you financially when you're up against it and don't see a way out?
- Do you trust God for your physical healing and trust He knows what He's doing if you don't see results right away?
- Do you trust Him to work good in tough relationships when you're completely out of ideas of what to try?
- Do you ask Him for help with a crazy work or school or home schedule and keep going with your head up and a good attitude?

Or do you spend a lot of time worrying and thinking over and over situations that may or may not have happened? Do you work hard trying to get things to turn out a specific way?

The steadfast of mind You will keep in perfect peace, because he trusts in You. Trust in the Lord forever. For in God the Lord, we have an everlasting Rock. Isaiah 26:3-4

Some trust in chariots and some in horses, but we trust in the name of the Lord our God. Psalm 20:7 NIV

One of my colleagues, Michelle, said something that resonates with me. "My most successful days are when I can live in the moment and trust Divine guidance in all action and inaction. I have come to understand that worry is the result of trying to live according to my own wisdom and thinking way too much. It is also synonymous with meditating on the ways I suspect God might be unfaithful."

If you trust in God, you won't have any trouble obeying. If you believe—if you choose to act as though what God says is true—then your actions will be congruous with your beliefs. If you still have trouble obeying, check what you really believe—the kinds of things you're thinking about.

Journal

One thing I've always had trouble acting on, even though I've said I believe it, is ____.

Other spiritual disciplines

Those are the most commonly recommended and practiced spiritual disciplines. Others include service, evangelism, stewardship, fasting, solitude, communion, confession. There are other ways you can stay tuned in to Jesus on a regular basis, like listening to praise and worship music throughout the day, listening to sermons and Christian teachers, or keeping a spiritual journal.

You can find some good information about these spiritual disciplines. Look for articles online by typing "spiritual disciplines" or "spiritual practices" into your search engine. You can find books about this by asking your pastor or a spiritual leader you trust for a suggestion, or by visiting a Christian bookstore or the library.

How to begin and maintain a life of faith

If you'd like to start your own faith habits but aren't sure where to begin, just remember, it doesn't have to be complicated. I suggest starting by getting into three new habits:

1. Get involved in a Bible-teaching church – both worship services and a small group of some type.
2. Pray about anything and everything.
3. Get into the Bible daily, in some fashion or other.

When you are already living life hard, maxing out every day without replenishing, the stressors of your days will compound burnout for you. From my own experience, I know when I am in HALT (Hungry-Angry-Lonely-Tired), I don't have the energy for anything and I sure don't feel like pursuing God. But, I also know that at these times, Satan will whisper all sorts of lies and rationalizations and distractions to keep me from praying or opening my Bible or centering my mind on God. Because the devil knows God is what I need the most, he's going to do anything he can to keep me from going there.

Satan will pound you with condemnation and guilt—and try to convince you that it won't work for you because you're such a lousy Christian you can't even do a five minute quiet time every day. Jesus will coax you with gentle, grace-filled reminders. Remember this difference—it's important!

The thief comes only to steal and kill and destroy; I came that they may have life, and have it abundantly. John 10:10

"Come to Me, all who are weary and heavy-laden, and I will give you rest. Take My yoke upon you and learn from Me, for I am gentle and humble in heart, and you will find rest for your souls. For My yoke is easy and My burden is light." Matthew 11:28-29

Go with Jesus' offer. It's a good invite!

It will take some personal self-discipline to make the choices to do these things and not default to other activities. But I promise it will eventually make a difference!

22

Discipline means to prevent everything in your life from being filled up. Discipline means that somewhere you're not occupied, and certainly not preoccupied. In the spiritual life, discipline means to create that space in which something can happen that you hadn't planned or counted on. ~Henri Nouwen

I'll admit that for a while, I told God at least once a day that "Church sucks." I used this strong language because I meant it, and you might relate. This is because the church—that group of people that gets together—is made up of broken people who are all in different places of figuring things out with God. No one fellowship is going to be able to heal anyone else. Broken people can do only do much. Some church fellowships are much better than others at coming alongside the wounded in positive ways. This is why, while, yes, you need to be in contact with other believers as part of finding your way, you can't put your hope and expectations on those people. Somehow, you'll be let down. Those people may be able encourage you and share some truth in the Bible to consider, but they can't change you. That's up to you and God.

It continues to amaze me how I functioned as well as I did keeping Jesus at arm's length for so long. My walk with Christ wasn't always superficial. I do remember some very precious times, like when I trusted God to help me as a single parent and when I had to open my heart and ask God to help me heal after the end of my first marriage. But it wasn't until I turned every aspect of my life to Jesus and began to let Him speak to me about true state of things in my heart that I began to experience victory and peace on a daily basis. I learned how to fight battles on a different level and began to win!

It doesn't matter what your relationship with Jesus looks like right now. It's never too late to turn your face to Him.

When You said, "Seek My face," my heart said to You, "Your face, O Lord, I shall seek." Psalm 27:8

Reminder

Experiment. If anything you try doesn't seem to work (after giving it a reasonable chance), it's OK to try something else. You can ask someone else what they do, but remember that just because it works for them, it isn't necessarily the right script for you to follow. Some people may try to tell you this or that is the only way a spiritual life is lived, the only version of the Bible you should read, the only way to pray, the only whatever. The truth is that there's only ONE way to be saved [see the short chapter at the end with that same title], and that's by believing that Jesus' death on the cross was sufficient to cleanse you from the guilt of your sin and that Jesus' resurrection to life again gives you eternal life. All the other musts and have-tos may or may not be so.

Ask God to show you the best ways for YOU, the way He wired YOU. He will show you as you continue to pursue Him. This is a prayer that He will answer because He delights in fellowship with you and wants you to find great enjoyment in His presence.

Reminder

Cut yourself some slack. Don't be hard on yourself if you forget or have to miss a day. The spiritual practices aren't about a whole new set of rules and must-dos to your busy day. This is about setting a firm foundation under your life and building a strong relationship with Jesus Christ. Ask God to bless what you can do and He will help you make it a priority.

Action

In the area of FAITH, I am going to _____.
I will do _____ by (a specific date) _____.

Prayer

Dear Jesus, I believe that You love me and that You see how much I'm struggling. Please help me to love You and learn the things I need to do to make my life more pleasing to you. Thank you for your death on the cross and for the power of Your Holy Spirit that makes working on myself even possible. I will expect great things with You! Amen

Check In

I'm sure I have accepted Jesus Christ's death in my place for my sins and I'm sure I have a place in heaven with God when I die.
— 100% sure
— I have some questions about this.
— What are you talking about?

I set aside time 3-5 times per week to pray, read my Bible and worship God for at least 30 minutes.
— Never
— Whenever I feel guilty enough
— Pretty regularly
— More than this

I meet with other believers to learn and worship
— Sunday morning, Sunday night and Wednesday night
— Sunday mornings
— Don't go to church

I have to admit I worry about things most of the time.
— True statement
— I can get going on one thing and it will ruin my day
— I'm pretty good at working through what's not worth worrying about but some things still bother me.

I'm satisfied with the way I handle my spiritual life. I know I could do better in a few areas, but for the most part, I'm doing pretty well.
— Nope, not even
— I have some good days, but I'm frustrated with myself a lot of the time
— On good days I can say this
— Yeah, a few things I'd like to do differently, but mostly, I'm in a good place.

Kay's story

Having been on my own for a while, I realize what a rich heritage my family gave to me. We didn't have a TV while I was in grade school, and while this was a source of grief to me, now I'm grateful for hours spent reading all the books I could carry home on our Saturday library trips. We lived out in the country, so when we got off the bus, entertainment was our own responsibility. I read and played outside and learned to appreciate my own company. While I would have liked to hang out with my friends in town sometimes, it also was a good excuse to skip a lot of the things that I knew I didn't want to do, like when those friends wanted to go drinking or drive to the next town after basketball games.

The one thing that I am more and more grateful for every day is exposure to Bible study and living according to God's wisdom. When he could, Dad would lead the family in some Bible lessons around the kitchen table. Sunday school and church were non-negotiable. In high school, my mom started leading those intense inductive Bible studies at the church, and I would sit in on them. Studying the Bible for myself, I learned about who God is, about His love for us, about the way He designed us to live.

I can identify a few pivotal points in my life along the way when I knew that I was at a crossroads. I could choose to do it God's way: forgive, maintain hope that things would get better, and keep doing the right thing I knew to do; or I could cling to my broken heart and trudge further into the darkness, trying to fix my hurt myself. I have never regretted giving up on my own efforts to fix my life. Through being single through my mid-forties, then getting married, and in starting a business and figuring out what success really is, God has been a precious and gracious Father. He will rebuke gently, pour out grace when I get tied up in self-pity and tantrums, and generally knock my socks off with generous love touches everywhere I turn. Sometimes I think back to those turning points and feel overwhelmed with gratitude that God got a hold of me early, so that I knew the only thing that would work was to hang on and submit to Him.

3 - FAMILY: A Family of a Different Kind

A happy family is but an earlier heaven. ~John
Bowring

My parents loved the five of us kids with their big, loving hearts, and there was always something going on and parts of our big extended Irish and Italian family over at the house. I have a lot of good memories of this ongoing madness, so much fun.

But...

The family was full of secrets and thoughtless hurts. My brothers would have to pull Dad off Mom in one of his drunk episode, but no one was allowed to mention the real reason Mom's eye was black. When I was five years old, my Mom and aunt were loading up for a trip to the zoo and forgot to put me in the car. They didn't figure it out until they were down the road a good way, and that became one of many seeds of fear planted during my growing up.

In our house, we didn't ask for help with our needs or hurts, and we certainly didn't seek help from outside the family, much less admit that something might be wrong. Your problems were your own fault (and their problems were likely your fault as well), so you figure it out.

The women were expected to keep the household running, doing all the work and putting their own needs aside for others, particularly for the guys, who didn't have the same rules. And no one could push back against this authority hierarchy without paying for it.

I had a severe speech impediment and other learning disabilities as a child. I didn't know how to use my voice, literally or figuratively. My sister had to speak for me. I learned early on that it was not OK to have problems or need something of anyone else—their issues were worse and more important than mine. Thus, no one in the family (or at school) pursued more than the one-size-fits-all special ed. classes for me, which got me, barely, through to graduation.

I know that things would have been different for me if my parents had known how to deal with their own brokenness, had known of any resources they could have used to cope with their struggles and pain. But they didn't know, and they weren't going to ask, so they did the best they could. I survived—wounded, not a warrior.

Your family can make or break you. There's no way around it: a healthy family is crucial for healthy growth and success in life. And a strong family is one of the best tools in your self-care toolbox for coping with life's ongoing stressors.

Journal

What's going through your mind right now when I bring up family—the healthy kind or the dysfunctional kind? Be honest with yourself and write down some thoughts. Then keep reading.

The importance of family

In 1989, the United Nations General Assembly formally recognized the family unit's unique status as the critical building block of civilized society. Some of the international consensus noted that "Families are the fullest reflection, at the grass-roots level, of the strengths and weaknesses of the social and developmental environment;" and "Families, as basic units of social life, are major agents of sustainable development at all levels of society, and their contribution is crucial for its success."[2]

From ancient times, civilization has acknowledged that family is the core unit of community. Family is where children are taught the "rules of engagement" for the culture into which they will grow. The family of origin is the first and the longest lasting influence upon a person and will impact behavior, belief, values, and expectations. The experiences in the home will shape the mental health, sense of integrity, and personal work ethic that a youngster will grow up with and take to the workforce and culture at large.

> *To put the world right in order, we must first put the nation in order; to put the nation in order, we must first put the family in order; to put the family in order, we must first cultivate our personal life; we must first set our hearts right. ~Confucius*

While the traditional family structure is undergoing significant cultural and political pressure in the United States and other nations, the fact remains that family was God's idea. God created Adam and Eve in His image and theirs was the first marriage (Genesis 2:18-25). They were instructed to procreate and fill the earth (Genesis 9:1, 6-7).

God went on to assign roles to husband, wife, dad, mom, and children. There are many, many Scripture passages in the New and the Old Testament that form a coherent picture of the family God desires. Long story short, we have a lot of instruction as to the leadership, example-setting, respect, selflessness, obedience, and love that are to be practiced in the family. Family units are the building blocks for successful communities, beneficial government (also established by God), and productive business and civic organizations, all of which in turn are supposed to further serve and build up strong and healthy families.

And God Himself is our Father, the ultimate picture of a father: *See how great a love the Father has bestowed on us, that we would be called children of God; and such we are.* 1 John 3:1. In this sense, Jesus Christ is our elder brother, who traveled the earth without sin and can show us the way. This whole picture itself is enough to encourage us to try to create the healthiest families we can, for our own sake and for those coming after us, our children and our communities.

Yeah, but MY family?

I can hear some of you brave and broken women, and see it on your faces. You're thinking, *All this talk about the ideal family situation is nice, but you don't know MY family. My family is NOT the example anyone wants to follow.*

I know, some of you come from families that were less than ideal. The grownups responsible couldn't create situations sufficient for basic physical safety and provision, much less for equipping children able to cope in a mad, mad world. My own family of origin was not at all healthy, and I learned a lot of bad coping mechanisms trying to grow up.

The reality is that your family may not be the kind of people you can fellowship with in a positive way. I don't begin to suggest you try to act as if your family is safe and healthy if they are not. If they refuse to see problems, if they insist you are the problem, if there is more going on there to tear you down than to build you up, then your family is not a tool in your self-care toolbox.

What are some ways to respond to this reality? Here are a few I can think of.

The Bible says to honor your parents as best you can.

Honor your father and your mother, that your days may be prolonged in the land which the Lord your God gives you. Exodus 20:12

Children, obey your parents in the Lord, for this is right. Honor your father and mother (which is the first commandment with a promise), so that it may be well with you, and that you may live long on the earth. Ephesians 6:1-3

There's a lot of debate as to what honoring parents means, especially when it comes to parents who deserve to be behind bars or those who are so dysfunctional that healthy seems weird. The world will offer a lot of ideas—all you have to do is visit the family self-help section of the nearest bookstore. And there might be some good information there, but let me say one thing: if you don't ask God to bring His wisdom into your situation and heal your heart, no amount of self-help from these books will be effective.

I had access to all these resources when I was trying to deal with my family and they did me no good. It took turning to seek God with no glossing over my issues. It took a firm commitment to obey Him. It took time in the Bible to renew how I thought and understand what He really means for families. God's perspective and God's ways are the only hope for a changed family that pleases Him.

"For My thoughts are not your thoughts, nor are your ways My ways," declares the Lord. "For as the heavens are higher than the earth, so are My ways higher than your ways and My thoughts than your thoughts." Isaiah 55:8-9

After seeking God, honoring your family may mean something like having meals with them and quietly letting them share their inappropriate opinions without finding ways to change the subject or being disagreeable about it. It may mean showing up for the family stuff and being as friendly as you can, but not engaging when the ugliness begins.

Honoring your parents does NOT mean you should obey them if they tell you to do something God clearly says is sin, like stealing or cheating. But maybe, if it isn't a matter of sin, you could do what they

31

want you to do, as a way of showing them respect? I know, it's a tricky call and no one answer will apply to every situation.

But I challenge you to pray and ask God to show you what loving and honoring your family can look like, even while you're praying for their salvation and restoration or whatever the case may be. I believe this is a prayer God will answer. From experience, I can tell you you'll be amazed at what He can do. At what He wants to do for you, because He loves you and your messed-up family. And because you desire to follow His instructions in honoring your mother and father.

A different family
You may have to find your own family.

For my father and my mother have forsaken me, but the Lord will take me up. Psalm 27:10

A father to the fatherless, a defender of widows, is God in his holy dwelling. God sets the lonely in families... Psalm 68:5-6

If you're unmarried and your family of origin is unbearable, create your own network and safety net. First of all, consider that Jesus Christ is your big brother, and God is your Father. Your relationship with God will be as rich and fulfilling as the effort you're willing to put into it. Then, who else can you add to your "family?"

I bet you already have friends who act as brothers or sisters, who make you laugh and irritate you just because they can, with whom you can have long, deep talks or just hang out in front of the TV. Be friendly with those around you and you never know when a wonderful new friendship will develop.

Where could you turn for role models, for wisdom in making decisions and coping with the crazy world? A pastor or an older Christian at your church whom you admire? A colleague at your work? If a relationship doesn't develop easily, consider asking someone you admire to mentor you, in a specific area or in your life in general.

Don't overlook your extended relatives who have managed to stay free of the family dysfunction. Even if they don't love the Lord, they do understand where you're coming from and might be able to help you deal with things.

Pray for God to bring you into a family. Be open to how He answers, because it might not look like you expect or want. But He knows what you need the most and He'll bring it about for you, because He loves you.

> *You must remember, family is often born of blood,*
> *but it doesn't depend on blood. Nor is it exclusive of*
> *friendship. Family members can be your best*
> *friends, you know. And best friends, whether or not*
> *they are related to you, can be your family.*
> *~Trenton Lee Stewart*

Journal

What does this do for you—the idea that family can be someone to whom you're not related? Name some people you'd love to add to your family.

The family you create

The family of choice is your chance to build strong relationships that please God and that serve as your port in the storm. If you are married, I encourage you to find a Bible-teaching church where you and your spouse can get involved with other Christian couples. Learn to strengthen your relationship with each other at the same time that you seek to raise your children in ways God can bless.

There are many excellent resources available for raising kids who love God and go into society to make a positive difference. When Mark, my second husband, and I got married, my son was five years old. While we both had our issues, as does every couple, we knew that we needed to be very deliberate about raising Will and creating a healthy family. We spent a lot of time looking at the Focus on the Family website (focusonthefamily.com) and others. There is a lot of excellent material out there for Christian parents who want to be sure they're creating a healthy and Godly environment, growing together spiritually, providing a safe place for kids to find answers and support as they venture out into the world.

While you can, mandate participation in Bible clubs or Christian scouting-type programs offered by many churches, which teach practical as well as intellectual and relational skills. Family camps are something we love to do. Here are two family camps to look into:

- Camp of the Woods: camp-of-the-woods.org
- Pine Cove: pinecove.com

Learn to practice unconditional love toward your kids while setting clear boundaries and expecting them to follow the rules. Listen to them and let them be who they are. Do your best to keep your home a physically and emotionally safe place free of negativity or violence or other unhealthy influences.

If you're not married yet, dear girl, be careful of your dating partners. Even if you are starved for love and attention, you will save yourself many regrets if you go slow and don't try to make just anyone fill that void. Don't rush into a relationship if you can see characteristics in him that you don't want to have to shield yourself or your children from later. Wait for the one God brings around in His time.

And if He doesn't bring you to marriage, you have the wonderful chance to press into God and live a great life filled with certain blessings and richness the married folks may be unable to pursue.

But I want you to be free from concern. One who is unmarried is concerned about the things of the Lord, how he may please the Lord;

but one who is married is concerned about the things of the world, how he may please his wife, and his interests are divided. The woman who is unmarried, and the virgin, is concerned about the things of the Lord, that she may be holy both in body and spirit; but one who is married is concerned about the things of the world, how she may please her husband. 1 Corinthians 7:32-24

For many years, work and school were the entire focus of my life. I worked, to the detriment of relationships, which were short-term and always ended in a bad blowup whenever they happened. My clients were my only relationships of substance, and it was a pretty poor substance. I managed to get married eventually, but this marriage resulted in an annulment because neither of us had a clue what God meant for marriage and family.

It wasn't until trying to raise my son as a single mom that I realized how much I needed the salvation of Jesus. My current husband and I work hard to make our family and home a place of acceptance and encouragement. We work on love and laughter every day, alongside the rules and chores and school and everyday life. We look to the Bible and seek God's wisdom—the design He put together—for a healthy and strong family.

Focus on your family

No family is perfect, because families are made up of imperfect people. But it is possible to share fun and laughter, encouragement, wisdom, and correction in ways that build up and strengthen rather than ways that tear down and destroy. The fact remains that the family is a vital and key building block to human development, and it should be nurtured and protected. More than ever, kids need to be taught how to be warriors out there, because the world will certainly wound them.

It takes work, commitment, and time in order to grow and maintain a healthy family. It is easy to focus on career, hobbies, and church activities, spending so much time outside the home we forget the ones we are closest to. I encourage you to practice making your family a priority. A strong family unit is a God-given refuge.

Here are some of the things my family has done and now do which bring us together.

- We had some conversations and created a family motto. "Hard work through Christ" is in a wooden frame on our kitchen wall. This is a great way to always remember it.
- We schedule a weekly family night around a meal, Bible time, or game. Each member of the family has a designated task. The kids love to have the responsibility of choosing a song, making dessert, reading the verses, and so on.
- We have set guideline about the usage of electronics, both in limits per day, and places or times during which phones, tablets, or games are not allowed. This is non-negotiable in order to fully enjoy quality family time.
- We take time to speak positively over each other. After dinner before everyone clears the table, everyone in the family states something positive about each of the others and about themselves as well. This is a fun and fulfilling way to be a family that builds each other up and creates shelter when things get tough out in the world!
- My husband and I often take time away from the kids and identify what is important for us in terms of core values, beliefs and personal behaviors we want to model before our kids and instill in them. At regular opportunities, we see ways to reinforce what is important through everyday life.
- Ask each child on a regular basis and find out from their perspectives what they like most about their family. Find a way to honor this during the following days.
- Pillow fights, nerf wars, games of tag, running through the sprinkler, spontaneous dancing, and singing, etc. It's important to not get so caught up in our schedules that we can't be silly and enjoy fun moments.
- We deliberately use mealtimes to bring up headlines or things happening at school or work to discuss them as a family and look at them in light of our values and beliefs. This has been good for us to understand what our kids are experiencing and how they are growing in their thinking and relationship with God.

Journal

List several things you would like to incorporate into your family routines. Remember to think about fun times as well as times to encourage and instruct each other.

Every day, when you're out doing errands, when you listen to the news and speak with those you rub shoulders, you see how crucial strong and healthy families are. A happy and safe family for yourself is one thing you can influence on your own behalf. It may seem too much to hope for, but pray and find a few small things you can do, and it will make a huge difference!

Reminder

When you're trying to make changes in your life, remember that you can only change yourself. No matter how much someone else may need to change, at the end of the day, you can't make them change. Focus on what you can do, such as responding in different ways to someone who pushes all your buttons.

Action

In the area of FAMILY, I am going to _____.
I will do _____ by (a specific date) _____.

Prayer

Dear Jesus, I believe that You love me and my family, no matter how messed up we might be. Please help me to look for ways to love my family members and be an example of You to them, but also to find the support and encouragement I need to do what I need to do for me. Thank you for wisdom in the Bible that can help point the way. I thank you for family! Amen

Here are some more resources where you can find more help in addition to pressing in to God. Whether it's a parent, a sibling, yourself or someone else in your family who is struggling with alcohol or drugs or any other kind of abuse, trauma and neglect, you will find help from those who have been exactly where you are.

- Alcohol abuse: al-anon.org
- Drug abuse: drughelpline.org
- Drug abuse: narconon.org
- Adult children of alcoholics and other kinds of family dysfunction: adultchildren.org
- Survivors of sexual abuse: rainn.org

Check In

My family sits down to eat dinner together
- — At least once a day most weeks
- — One to three times a week if we're lucky
- — It may happen by chance, but we don't plan it.

We do things as a family, like play games around the table, play sports together or exercise, cook or just sit and talk
- — We're always planning stuff to do together; I wish we'd cut back a bit.
- — Maybe once a week.
- — Once a month, if someone does the planning and nagging.
- — Ha ha, wouldn't that be nice?

We go to church together
- — Once a week
- — Once a month
- — Christmas and Easter, faithfully
- — Never

We discuss things as a family and work stuff through
- — Yes, it's how we handle life
- — We get together whenever a crisis hits
- — Discuss things? As a family? And work out solutions? Is that possible?

We talk about God and the Bible and issues of faith as a family.
- — All the time
- — When it's important enough to resort to religion
- — Only as swear words and narrow-minded commentary

Laura's story

Since I've started college, I've found it absolutely necessary to make time in the day to relax and destress, whether it be to watch something on TV or hangout with my friends. In doing this I let my mind kind of refresh in a way. Through my two years of college, so far, I have been met with many strenuous days and nights, but I've always made sure my mental health is in check before taking up any major task. In doing this, I also have learned that eating good food and exercising never fails to bring me back to a place of center and well-being. Also, I have relied on my support system of faith, friends, and family to get me through my hardest days.

Whenever I don't make room for myself by using excuses like "I don't have enough time," or "I have so much on my plate this extra thing isn't necessary," I quickly realize that my mind and body are not the same without these forms of self-care. By taking care of myself first, even if it's 30 minutes out of the day, I'm able to refocus and reboot my mind and body.

There have been many times that I have felt wounded throughout my life, but college has shown me some of the deepest lows that I have ever had to face. Being met with high expectations for school and relationships, yet also trying to remain healthy mentally and physically is not just exhausting, but it is also a true test of character. Although this is a reality, I've also felt like a warrior in that I have overcome these obstacles day in and day out. I continue to use self-care, faith, family, and friends to help guide me through the goals that I have always wished to achieve.

4 - FOOD: Food For Thought

You are what you eat.

Now before you say "Yeah, yeah," to that, ask yourself this question: Do you live to eat or eat to live?

Here's the difference: If you live to eat, you value food as more than simply fuel. One of the purest pleasures you can imagine might be eating out with friends, a huge traditional holiday feast with family, or a romantic date over a specially prepared meal.

Living to eat might also mean food is a means of comfort or control.

Eating to live, on the other hand, implies eating in order to live well, enjoying all things in moderation and making the kinds of diet choices which lend to a longer and healthier life.

So, let me ask again: Are you eating to live or living to eat? What is food to you?

One of my lifetime coping mechanisms for the stress I lived with was an inappropriate relationship with food.

41

I struggled with being overweight since I was nine. My mother was Italian, and this translated into a huge culture of love being equated with food. Family = love = food. "Eat, eat, eat!" was the way "I love you!" was said around my house. In addition to this pressure, I was incapable of eating white flour and sugary foods in moderation. After having one bite, the bite had me! I had to eat it all. I obsessed about those refined carbs and developed physical cravings for them.

Years later, my breaking point was despair, depression, and thoughts about suicide. I was 200 pounds, unable to keep up the activity of daily living and I couldn't lose weight on my own. Sick and tired of being sick and tired, I recognized my own addictive behaviors, but I was powerless and hopeless, afraid to live and desperate for help.

At the recommendation of a therapist, I finally tried a 12-step group and began to understand I had addictive and emotional issues in addition to food triggers that caused intense cravings I could not refuse. A lot of soul searching led me to a new relationship with Jesus Christ, which was what my broken heart was really craving. Along the way, I gave up white flour and sugar, which freed me from the physical cravings and the mental obsessions that kept me bound in my miserable, addictive cycle.

Stress and food

Our relationship with food is one of the most visible ways our stress manifests. Food is plentiful and usually easy to get in this country, so it's no surprise it's one of the easiest things to lose oneself in. Let's take a look at a few of the problems that can crop up around food when it comes to stress and work.

In the fight or flight mechanism triggered by stressful situations, the initial response of the brain is to release hormones to suppress the appetite. The body gets ready for the high activity of fight or flight, so eating is not a priority. When the stress continues, or when the body perceives the "danger" is ongoing, stress hormones now (among other actions) increase the appetite. This is because now the body wants the energy to fuel the fight or flight.

Under stress, we tend to reach for fat- and sugar-heavy items. Science indicates that the sugar and fat interrupt the stress-hormone producing loop, introducing a measure of comfort.[10] So chronic stress not only triggers the need to eat, it also seems to want to consume the things which are least healthy.

Weight issues
Carrying this line of thought further, high and constant levels of stress can lead to weight issues. Many studies implicate diets high in fat and sugar in weight gain. Being too busy to find a healthy meal is one contributor, when it's easier to grab a candy bar out of the vending machine or stop by the fast food place on the way to the next obligation. Vending machines and fast food restaurants are not the best places to find the healthier options.

Too much sugar also contributes to creation of fat when the liver converts excess glucose to fat and sends it into storage for later need. But under continual stress and continual supply of calories, your body never needs to tap into those reserves, so the pounds pack on. Sugar consumption also releases insulin. Insulin will shut off the body's fat burning mechanism and take advantage of the more easily accessed sugar in the bloodstream. Fat not consumed plus more sugar coming through equals more fat in storage.

> *Pasta doesn't make you fat. How much pasta you*
> *eat makes you fat. ~Giada De Laurentiis*

Diabetes and cardiovascular issues
While the cause of insulin resistance is widely debated, diets that are high in simple carbohydrates and saturated fats are strongly implicated in diabetes. And while consumption of sugar does not lead directly to diabetes, a diet high in fat and sugar, and the accompanying obesity issues, will contribute to the development of Type 2 diabetes.

Obesity, of course, is highly implicated in heart disease and stroke risk.

Skipping meals

Another example of stress-related poor eating choices is skipping meals. Skipping meals leads first to depleted energy, brain fog and lack of concentration. This is just not workable when you're stressed out already and trying to function. What could happen? According to a National Motor Vehicle Crash Causation Survey, recognition and decision errors accounted for 74% of vehicle accidents.[11] A moment of inattention could result in serious injury or death. At work, a brain-fogged decision could mean financial repercussions, strained work relationships, loss of job, or simply more stressful situations. At the very least, functioning while depleted will serve to keep you at a level of life that you don't like.

And when you finally sit down to eat, chances are that you will overeat. Cycles of starvation and then overeating put immense loads on your body's ability to regulate energy levels, hormones, and mood.

You've heard it before, and I'm going to say it again: Skipping breakfast is bad for you. You may think you don't have time for breakfast. But do you have time for low energy, brain fog, poor concentration, feeling famished way before lunchtime, a bad mood, poor memory, fatigue? On the other hand, think what a good portion of protein, a little good fat, a serving of whole grains and a piece of fruit could do for your day. Lots of energy, great attention span, clear thinking, better productivity, and not hungry all day then overeating later.

Journal

Reread the parts above about stress-related food choices and skipping meals and write a few honest lines about this: Could any part of your daily stress level be caused by skipping breakfast? List the things you'll add to your breakfast options.

Poor nutritional choices

As I already mentioned, our food choices tend to be less than ideal when we're stressed and busy. We go for fast food because it's fast, and choose prepared and frozen meals to microwave because they're easy. All of it is usually tasty and comforting.

The problem with fast food—by which I mean most of the restaurants lining the streets these days—and prepared, packaged meals at the grocery store, is what they're made of. Fast foods are typically loaded with sodium, trans fats, carbohydrates/sugar, artificial sweeteners, and preservatives. Excess amounts of these on a regular basis over time contribute to a host of health problems: headaches, elevated blood pressure, water retention, dental problems, acne, weight gain, blood sugar spikes and insulin resistance, diabetes, digestive and bowel issues, elevated cholesterol, weight gain, heart disease, stroke risk, cancer, asthma, allergies, neurologic problems.

Even fast foods that appear healthy, for example, made with whole grains, or packaged under the labels "natural" or "low calorie" are most likely still compromised in terms of sodium, fat, and carbohydrate content.

These are just the most visible outcomes of a fast food diet. Many stressed and busy people struggle with nutritional and hormonal deficiencies caused by their repeated poor food choices. Fast foods and processed foods in packages, cans, and microwaveable containers are usually low in the vitamins, minerals, healthy fats, and other building blocks the body needs to build healthy tissues and work at peak performance.

Individuals can struggle with low energy, brain fog, depression, weakness, compromised immunity, or poor bone structure, all due to nutritional deficiency.[12] A number of foods sold today also contribute to disruption of hormone production in the body, either because of the artificially enhanced conditions in which the food substances are produced or because of the way these substances interfere with natural food digestion in the body. I'm thinking of alcohol, gluten, dairy, soy, sugar, factory-processed animal products, nightshades, and "white" foods (bread, potatoes, pasta, etc.)[13]

For the busy career woman, wife, mom, teacher, student…these convenient foods are convenient and yummy! However, they will take their toll on you eventually. Here is a list of the things I personally avoid and will go so far as to say everyone should avoid.

- **Sugar added**, whether it's white processed, honey, turbinado or otherwise, is rarely necessary for good-tasting food. The food just gets sweeter with no nutritional gain. Once you wean yourself off of sugar, you'll discover how great things taste on their own!

- **Trans fats or hydrogenated fats** (not natural unsaturated fats) increase bad cholesterol, impacting insulin resistance and heart disease and other problems. Trans and hydrogenated fats are manmade products designed to increase shelf life; they are not natural. They are not worth the risk.[14]

- By **white foods or refined carbs**, I mean white bread or anything made out of processed white flour, white rice, potatoes, and pasta. These are loaded with simple carbs with low nutrient levels.

- Science has come up with all kinds of **preservatives and food additives** to keep foods in their bright and alluring packaging from spoiling on the shelves. They are approved by the FDA, but there is little real research to prove they are not harmful. In fact, there's more research coming in that says they can cause neurological damage and contribute to allergies and cancers.[15]

- **Artificial sweeteners** were designed to make sodas and other foods sweet without the calories, but like the preservatives, they are proving to lead to serious health complications, such as metabolic syndrome,[16] headaches, mood disorders, weight gain, cancer, organ dysfunction, gastrointestinal distress, and other problems.[17] Real sugar would be better, which tells you how much I dislike artificial sweeteners.

- **Dairy** – Milk, cheese, yogurt, and ice cream… These, as commercially produced in the United States, are full of hormones, pesticides, antibiotics, sugar and fat, which are NOT good for you. And while the USDA promotes its new food pyramid, science is still undecided as to whether dairy has any nutritional benefit for us adults, or whether it's the calcium that we need, which can be obtained other ways.

- **High fructose corn syrup** is everywhere, but your body wasn't made to deal with it in excessive amounts. It turns easily into fat, which problems we've already discussed in terms of obesity, heart problems and so on.[18]

You may already know of your own problem food, or you may be suspecting something. If not, this list is a good place to start experimenting. Read labels and begin eliminating things from your diet. Take notes as to how you feel, what kind of energy you gain, headaches or skin problems that clear up—or any other changes you notice.

While I encourage you to avoid these on the basis of questionable health benefits, I want to say again that it's different for everybody. You may be just fine with caffeine or white flour. Or you may have a food sensitivity or reaction that triggers a health issue or overeating. Be aware of what you're eating and know what it does to you and for you.

Journal

What would you like to try eliminating from your diet for a while? What do you think it will do for you?

Emotional eating and overeating

Overeating is a socially acceptable behavior in our culture. In fact, it can even be encouraged throughout holidays or life events. Think about all the food associated with Thanksgiving, Christmas, Valentine's Day, Memorial Day, Halloween, birthday parties, weddings, funeral dinners, family reunions. Church pot-lucks and company dinners also feature too much food. Even an outing to the average restaurant can serve up monster portion sizes.

It's hard to eat in moderation when all the dishes are spread out and everything looks so good and nobody's counting how many times you get up and get another plate. We all rationalize going back up for seconds: "It's the holidays," "I don't eat this kind of thing very often." "Aunt Julie will feel bad if she doesn't see me eating her pecan pie." "I'll diet later." And it's hard when it's Grandma or Mom filling your plate again—we need to not cause a scene by implying the food's not good or whatever the case may be in your particular family dynamics. Overeating is easy because company is always better around food.

What goes through your head when you overeat? Enjoying a second helping at a big family dinner probably won't hurt you if it's only once in a while. However, if you find yourself overeating repeatedly, even when you don't want to, and when certain kinds of thoughts circle in your mind, you may be dealing with a food addiction.

Do you eat when you're not hungry or eat until you feel uncomfortable or sick?

Do you reach for food when your emotions are running high and you need to stop feeling?

Do you eat differently by yourself than when you are around others? Have others commented on your eating in ways that tell you they see problems?

Do you feel ashamed or embarrassed about the way you eat or look? Do your eating habits impact other areas of your life, like running low on cash because you're always at the drive-thru, or skipping appointments or meetings because you're eating?

Do you have health problems related to your eating habits?

Do your thoughts revolve around food—ways to avoid having to eat, getting more food, counting calories, wishing food wasn't so important to you, or hating the way you handle food?

Do you feel that you deserve food because you had a bad day or deserve to be able to avoid feeling the way you feel?

48

Do you crash diet, only to regain the weight immediately, or use laxatives, vomiting, lots of exercise or other methods to try to lose weight?

These and other signals may help make it clear whether you have a food addiction. Check out these websites for more information that may be helpful.

- Overeaters Anonymous: oa.org Use the Find a Meeting feature to find a meeting near you, or click on the Are you a Compulsive Overeater? link near the top for more questions to ask yourself.
- Food Addicts: foodaddicts.org Click on Am I a Food Addict? under the New to FA tab.

Journal

Go ahead and spend some time writing down your answers to the questions above. Check out the websites for more questions. What do you think? Is it time to get help with a deeper issue around food that you can't control anymore?

There's a lot of wisdom in developing a habit of awareness of your thoughts and emotions around food. Whether you're eating with others or by yourself, learn to recognize the kinds of food you're eating and the kinds of things that go through your mind while you're eating or thinking of getting more food. Emotional eating leads to all the health issues we've already talked about, but it is also a clue there are larger issues in your life that could use some healthier coping skills. Your issue might be a simple biochemical food trigger instead of an emotional trigger, which sets off a phenomenal craving that leads you into overeating.

If you already know what your eating triggers are, you can determine to find other ways to respond to whatever it is making you uncomfortable. If you're bored, do something else you enjoy, like reading, hiking, working on a hobby. If you're exhausted, take a long luxurious bath or have a cup of hot herbal tea. If it's a hard relationship, consider seeking counsel from a wiser person or a professional counselor. If you're anxious, take a brisk walk or practice calming breathing exercises.

If you're not sure what prompts your emotional eating, or if you're afraid to try to change things by yourself, seek help. You know the benefits will far outweigh the hard work of figuring things out and changing your food habits.

Don't dig your grave with your own knife and fork.
~English Proverb

The problem with diets
While we're talking about food, we have to bring up the subject of diets. The term engenders the concept of deprivation and frustration, which has never seemed like a good foundation for successful weight control to me.

Diets that focus on calorie restriction or forbidding certain types of foods don't work. Here are a couple of reasons why:

When your body experiences prolonged calorie deprivation, it responds by lowering the metabolic rate in order to gain the most energy from what is consumed. When the diet is over, if you return to normal eating patterns, your body is all of a sudden getting plenty. Any weight you lost is now rapidly regained at the lower metabolic rate.

Another reason is that after a while, the dieter will begin to crave whatever is being denied. Physically, nutritional deficiencies may occur, so the body craves what will right the imbalance. Psychologically, the desire to have what one "can't" have can be quite strong. The diet is abandoned, and giving up is usually accompanied by guilt, self-resentment and more negative stress you don't need.

There are myriad weight loss aids in the form of diet pills, herbal supplements, or prescription drugs. Some of these are harmless and do not affect weight at all, except perhaps the weight of your wallet. Some may have the actual effect of reducing appetite, increasing the feeling of fullness, increasing metabolism or other effects. However, they can also contain substances which cause other serious problems like elevated heart rate and blood pressure, anxiety, digestive problems, sleep interruptions, and organ damage.[19] A number of diet aids have been banned after people became quite ill or even died because of diet pill use. If you take an over-the-counter diet pill, you have no way of knowing what ingredients are going into your body.

I ask you to avoid fad diets and weight loss supplements if you want to lose weight. I do not believe the benefits are better than the risks of harm to your body, particularly fast weight loss programs. If you want to lose weight, or if you want to develop a healthy relationship with food, I urge you to begin a mindful look at food and your lifestyle around it.

The problem with eating healthy

When we are depleted and have exhausted ourselves, life becomes one big chore and we have no kind of energy or stamina. It's easy to go for the quick fix and use food as a way to alter brain chemistry. Foods particularly high in sugar and fat produce an instant change in sugar levels for immediate gratification. Not falling into this kind of trap boils down to forming good food-related habits in order to avoid this stress-related eating. This, however, means deliberate and careful work. And I understand—nobody has time for that. However, not making the time for it is setting yourself up for more serious problems down the line.

I like the saying, "Failing to plan is planning to fail." Healthy eating is about planning out your food ahead of time and making it as easy as possible. A lot of people argue that this takes too much time, but stop and think for a minute. What happens when you stop whatever you are doing and go grab a quick bite? It takes time and pulls you away from your task, so you lose your momentum and you lose more productive time getting back into the flow. The type of food planning I mean has snacks ready so you don't have to quit to eat, and menus planned and shopping done so you don't lose time trying to figure of what to fix.

My family has given me the nickname of "snack fairy" because I always have some kind of food available at all times. I am always prepared with a water bottle and snacks. When I used to drive up to Pittsburgh and visit my mom, my sister would always comment about my healthy eating. Wherever I go, students, friends, and coworkers ask about my meals on-the-go. Many people want to eat healthy but encounter difficulty starting something new. Being busy and not knowing how to prepare fast easy meals-to-go are the typical obstacles to eating healthy.

You can do it, though. It will take some new and careful effort, but once you get the hang of it, it's so easy!

Your diet is a bank account. Good food choices are good investments. ~Bethenny Frankel

First, spend some time studying nutrition basics. If you don't already have a good idea, learn about the different food groups and about things like proteins and complex carbohydrates, good fats and bad fats. Figure out how to read food labels and get a good food encyclopedia that has nutrition profiles, how to buy, store, and prepare different kinds of fresh meats, vegetables, fruits and other foods.

Learn the difference between real or natural food sources and the rest. The ideal stuff comes to you in the form it was created in—it grew out of the ground, or moved around the earth, sea, or sky. I'm talking vegetables, fruits, whole grains, nuts, eggs. These foods are generally found around the outside perimeter of the grocery store.

Some processing is required to get certain food to you: meat, fish, poultry, dairy products. Some flash frozen foods like fruits and veggies are minimally processed. These may or may not be OK, depending on what the guidelines you decide to adopt for yourself.

Processed foods are in the aisles, and they are found in cans, boxes, packages, and bags. They are snacks, sweets, and fully prepared meals. Their labels list all kinds of ingredients you can't pronounce and sound like chemicals. These ingredients are the preservatives they put in to make it last longer, the additives they use to give it an appealing look and texture, and the fats, sugars, and sodium they put in to make it taste so, so good. These substances are the ones the body has such a hard time with, which contribute to weight gain and health problems. These are the ones to avoid. Read through the list above again and learn to recognize these ingredients on food labels.

If you can't pronounce it, don't eat it. ~Common sense

You can go vegetarian (no meat, but eggs, milk, and cheese are OK). You can go vegan (no animal product whatsoever). I don't advocate one over the other, but I do encourage you to experiment and see which diet makes you feel the best. God wired everyone differently.

There are countless food lifestyles and meal plans out there, and sorting through them can be overwhelming. Is your goal simply eating better? Find a Mediterranean diet cookbook and browse through to see if it's appealing. If you're wanting to lose weight at the same time, look for a book to help you make low-fat but tasty meal and snack plans. Once you have some ideas, you have something to try and then tweak according to what your goals are and what actually works for your style and needs.

At the end of the book, I've included the daily meal plan that I tend to follow. It has suggestions for basic food group portions and a few easy recipes. This is what works for my body and lifestyle. Feel free to copy and change it up!

A few tips
Don't forget to take these things into consideration while you're looking at diet plans or cooking styles. What you have to work with will inform what you decide to do.

- Your food budget
- Your health issues
- The time you can devote to meal prep
- The kind of support you'll want or need

If you've tried diets before, remember why you quit. What was going on there that you can watch out for, to avoid repeating or to try again with better understanding or support?

Consider how the diet plan treats your own sacred cows—ice cream, chips, cake...whatever it is you cannot say no to. Will you need to cut it off completely, or is there room to indulge a little? Work with what you know will be best for your style. The better the fit, the greater your chance of success.

Keep a diary of new things you've been trying and how things work out. Be sure to record all your wins—a new favorite recipe everyone loves, a great new snack you can carry in your pocket and eat in a few minutes to get you through the afternoon slump. Take note of things that don't work so well also, but try to focus on what's working, because that's where you'll find your results.

Two final thoughts

If you have straightened up your diet and been exercising for a while, yet still struggle with fatigue, brain fog, or poor mood and motivation, it may be time to ask your doctor for a nutritional panel, which involves a complete blood count (CBC) and complete metabolic panel (CMP). These simple blood tests can tell you if you are functioning with deficiencies or imbalances. Most insurance plans cover these tests if your doctor orders them.

While you may need a supplement to restore an imbalance quickly, I am not of the opinion that you will need regular dietary supplements if you are eating a good array of veggies, fruits, and whole grains. If you do opt to use supplements, check with your doctor and then look for lab-tested products you can be sure are safe.

*If you don't take care of your body, where are you
going to live? ~Unknown*

I don't believe you can't enjoy good food. Food is a gift from God, and there's nothing wrong with enjoying a tasty meal. However, eating as well as you can is critical to treating your body as a sacred place for the living power of the Holy Spirit to reside. Habits of over-indulgence reflect a lack of self-control, while eating to numb the pain denies Jesus Christ the chance to help you work through your problems and find Godly ways to cope. On the other hand, slavish adherence to the best diet in the world does not increase your holiness. Be deliberate about finding the balance that helps you to feel and function the best, but still enjoy life. This balance is what it takes to do your best, at play and at work.

All things are lawful for me, but not all things are profitable. All things are lawful for me, but I will not be mastered by anything. 1 Corinthians 6:12

For everything created by God is good, and nothing is to be rejected if it is received with gratitude; for it is sanctified by means of the word of God and prayer. 1 Timothy 4:4-5

Reminder

Keep it as simple as possible. If you find yourself getting discouraged because the recipes are too exotic or complicated, look for something easier. I personally keep small bags of ready-to-eat snacks on hand all the time, with my water bottle. Also, I eat every 3-4 hours, focusing on proteins, veggies, and healthy fats.

Reminder

Giving yourself permission to be flexible, remembering that sticking to the overall plan is essential to success. Be sure to give it enough time to really show how it's going to play out. For example, if your new plan calls for you to eliminate all dairy, give your body a couple weeks to process out the accumulated whatever it's been building up from all

55

that dairy. Don't give up if you initially start to feel worse right away rather than better. Wait for your body to find the new normal and see how you feel.

Action

In the area of FOOD, I am going to _____.
I will do _____ by (a specific date) _____.

Prayer

Dear Jesus, I believe that You love me, no matter what shape my body is in. Please help me to make wise decisions around food and build healthier habits into my life. Thank you that it is within my power to do things to make myself healthier and enjoy life more. This is an amazing body You designed for me! Amen

Check In

I find myself eating when I am (check all that apply)
- — Stressed out
- — Tired
- — Bored
- — Angry
- — Lonely
- — A little snacky
- — Ravenous
- — When the clock says it's time to eat
- — I have to remember to eat, usually after wondering why I'm fatigued, jittery, irritable, brain- fogged or some combination thereof.

I eat until
- — My tummy is comfortable.
- — Everyone else stops eating.
- — I'm bloated and I hate myself.
- — The bag/carton/ serving bowl/ platter is empty.

I eat home cooked dinners and pack my own lunches
- — Every day
- — When I have time, otherwise it's fast food.
- — I don't have time to cook but I buy healthy meal-sized options to fashion a meal with on the go.
- — Fast food is king.

To me, a diet is
- — Taking care to avoid foods that are fatty, salty, sugary and otherwise bad for me, and eating plenty of things that are good for me, so I can feel good.
- — Any way I can lose a fast 15 pounds to look good dressed up for a special occasion.
- — A depressing battle of will-power, hunger and crabbiness, until I give up – again.

Which of the following do you eat daily?
- — Simple carbs
- — Trans fats or hydrogenated fats
- — Sweets
- — Fried foods
- — Salty snacks
- — Artificial sweeteners
- — Fruits
- — Vegetables
- — Animal proteins

Emma's story

I remember when my mom sat me down while I had tears swelling in my eyes. She told me she knew something was wrong and that I needed to get better. I realized that my hatred for my body and my relationship with food was toxic, but I was scared of recovery and all that it entailed.

My mom came up with a game plan and found me a nutritionist. Soon after, I had my first meeting with the nutritionist. I remember sitting down with her and feeling waves of anxiety because I knew that the feeling of control over what I ate and how much I ate was about to be shattered. I was shocked when I realized how much I had sabotaged my body and health, and I started to realize that I needed change, not only for my current being, but my future self.

The next weeks and months, I struggled to find the light in recovery. Challenging my damaging behaviors and trying to pursue a better mindset and positivity was an exhausting struggle. Soon though, I discovered that with my consistent work, happiness was coming easier and my bad habits started to dwindle. Of course, I had good days and bad days, but the good days started to outnumber the bad little by little.

I found joy in allowing myself to eat food that I once told myself was not allowed. I found joy in being able to go on dates with my boyfriend at the time without worrying about how many calories I was eating. I found joy in being more spontaneous with my friends, and I found joy in truly believing the affirming words of Jesus.

Once I gave up my eating disorder, I found myself. Before, I was a lost, insecure, rigid, and unhappy girl, but now, I have bloomed into a confident, sassy, compassionate, and Jesus loving-girl. I am able to see that God has made beauty from the ashes of my eating disorder.

5 - FITNESS: Getting a Move On

For me, fitness has to include the dimension of physical exercise. It started out of desperation: I began getting up and being at the gym at 4:30 in the morning. This was literally the only time I had to pray and not be actively coping with some very intense demands when Lily first came home. But since those days of basic survival, some very fruitful habits have woven their way into my life, without which I now don't think I could cope. Alongside the physical benefits of the discipline—feeling great!—I also spend precious hours with God, mulling over His goodness and seeing how to get through the day. My exercise time was the cooking pot in which this book simmered for a long time!

Fitness and food are closely related when it comes to a body functioning as it was designed to, enabling us to live life well. Excellent nutrition optimizes the engine we have, and physical fitness optimizes the mechanics of our body, how well we can move and get things done. The two work in tandem for the best possible health.

However, stress does a great deal to inhibit the fascinating machinery God designed.

One of the definitions of stress in the Google dictionary is "a state of mental or emotional strain or tension resulting from adverse or demanding circumstances." Any situation outside our own control or not going the way we want would be stressful:

- Sitting in a traffic jam when you're late
- Hating the job you're late for
- Seeing someone else mistreated and being unable to intervene
- Trying to get work done with inadequate resources and a frustrating boss
- Getting home to find your children have trashed the house and your husband didn't notice—again
- Not being able to go to sleep at night because your upstairs neighbor wears concrete flip-flops and loves to dance

Stress and the body

As mentioned in the previous chapter, the stress reaction is a good thing, created by God to equip human beings to handle threats of physical danger by escaping or fighting back. You do want that surge of adrenaline when you see a large dog rushing at you, or a see the baby crawling toward the top of the stairs. However, at some point, the stress reaction becomes a bad thing.

Your body cannot tell the difference between a mental threat and an actual physical threat, and it takes 20-60 minutes for the average body to reset from the rush of adrenaline and noradrenaline. Therefore, if you are continually exposed to stressful situations, your body perceives that you are constantly under attack and keeps on obliging you with the means to fight or flee. Living in chronic stress, your body cannot fully recover from the adrenaline rush before it is triggered again, and this will build up serious health risks. Does any of this sound familiar?

- Rapid breathing, shortness of breath, dizziness, fatigue, and loss of concentration.
- Increased heart rate and blood pressure damage which both arteries. Stress-related coping behaviors like smoking, alcohol consumption, poor eating habits and lack of physical activity

create other problems that increase the risk of heart attack and stroke, like high cholesterol and clogged arteries.[3]

- Frequent sickness, infection and slower healing due to compromised immune system.[4] That compromise also creates chronic inflammation leading to pains and tissue damage.
- Poor sleep or insomnia—lack of sleep boosts stress hormones, which makes it even harder to sleep.[5]
- Type 2 diabetes or high blood sugar. Your liver releases extra glucose with which to fight or flee stress, and constant high levels of blood sugar are prime for developing type 2 diabetes or experiencing a dangerous elevation of sugar levels.[6]
- Tension headaches, backaches, strains, and other pains from chronically tensed muscles.
- Heartburn, esophageal spasms, constipation and other gastric discomfort. Chronic stress can impair the way food moves through your intestines and how well nutrients are absorbed. Stress also affects your metabolism.[7]
- Stress can negatively impact sexual health and performance by decreasing libido, interfere with sexual arousal in men and disrupt the monthly cycle in women.[8]

Journal

List the major stresses you experience on a regular basis. Now list the ways you feel stress physically. Constant fatigue? Heartburn? Headaches all the time? What relationships do you notice between the two, if any?

There are many healthy ways to cope with stress. We've talked about developing your relationship with God, learning to rely on Him to show you how to respond to things and to meet your needs. We've talked about nurturing or creating a family with whom to shelter from stress and enjoy down time and encouragement. We've talked about good food as a way to get the proper energy you need to cope with the very real negative impacts of a high-stress life. Now I want to talk about fitness as an effective way to deal with the physical impacts of stress.

> *Training gives us an outlet for suppressed energies created by stress and thus tones the spirit just as exercise conditions the body. ~Arnold Schwarzenegger*

God made your body, you fabulous woman. You are fearfully and wonderfully made (Psalm 139). I'm continually amazed when I read books and articles about how things work in the body—about the fascinating ways God made our bodies to function, to heal, and to compensate!

Therefore I urge you, brethren, by the mercies of God, to present your bodies a living and holy sacrifice, acceptable to God, which is your spiritual service of worship. Romans 12:1

While largely suggesting that we use our physical bodies to do the tasks of kingdom building, it would not be out of place to say this verse also encourages doing what it takes to keep these earthly vehicles in proper working order—so we can be effective in the physical work we do. Ephesians 2:10 reminds us that *We are His workmanship, created in Christ Jesus for good works, which God prepared beforehand so that we would walk in them.* We need strong, healthy bodies with which to carry out the Great Commission, if we can do anything about it at all.

I believe we are to stay as healthy as possible as a witness and glory to God--taking care of what He has given us in order to do the tasks He has given us. In Genesis 1, God said "Very good!" when He finished creating man, so it would be good stewardship to take care of what pleases Him. Also, I'm just so grateful for all God has done for me, and I feel part of what I can do to show my gratitude is to take the best care I can of what He gave me, including my body.

I like to move it, move it!*

*In the words of King Julian (the original Madagascar movie)

We've talked about good nutrition, and I don't have to say much about getting enough good sleep—in short: few people get enough and we know it's important. Now I want to focus on a personal exercise routine which you can create and use to attain your best physical fitness and mental health.

Aerobic exercise—which increases the heart rate, moves your major muscle groups and makes you sweat—will have a dramatic impact on you. In the physical realm, those stress hormones are reduced, while the body's natural painkillers and mood lifters are released. Your heart, your endurance, your strength, your metabolism, and your pants size undergo transformations. You'll come to love the exhilaration and calm you get from exercising, once you get past the tougher beginning stages.

The overall effects of regular, vigorous exercise have been recognized as beneficial against depression and anxiety disorders.[9] At the very least, you can enjoy being away from all your sources of stress a few times every week.

It is also important to remember the other types of exercise besides aerobic and incorporate them into your workout routine. Weight lifting increases your strength and your lean muscle mass, which is important during weight loss efforts. Flexibility exercises like stretching will increase your range of motion, which reduces chance of injury during other activities. Don't forget movements designed to increase your balance.

Imagine feeling good physically again. You can like the body you're in, and you can feel good about the mastery and self-discipline you're developing. Your self-confidence will go up, and this renewed sense of energy and confidence will help you find more purpose in everything else you do. I don't begin to suggest that you have to get up and exercise at 4:30 in the morning! I do suggest that you try something potentially drastic if it's the only way to bring good exercise habits into your routine! You never know what it might bring for you.

You crazy-busy moms, 4:30 am might be your secret weapon!

A 20-minute walk can help you work the kinks out and help you to refocus. However, I want to encourage you to find something you can do to make yourself sweaty and exhausted a few times a week. I am referring to activities like running, biking, swimming, spinning, walking, hiking, dancing, cross-country skiing, kickboxing, aerobics classes, and the cardio machines at the gym.

You may be more intrigued by less vigorous activities like Pilates, yoga, or tai chi. These forms of exercise are less taxing in terms of long-term endurance, but they can be just as beneficial in terms of strength, flexibility, and balance. They will give you the same definite health and physical benefits as well as the same mental focus, mood elevation, and de-stressing.

Journal
What do you imagine you'd feel like if you did develop an exercise regimen? Write down a couple things you think would be different in your body. Now write down three honest reasons you don't exercise regularly.

Those who think they have no time for exercise will
sooner or later have to find time for illness.
~Edward Stanley

Those Eastern exercises
I've taught yoga for eight years now. Many Christians have concerns about practicing yoga or tai chi or other forms of exercise originating

in the East. Former practitioners warn Christians about the spirits involved in posing the body and meditating as guided by instructors.

Here's my response to this: I believe our bodies are God's perfect creation and keeping my body healthy honors Him. He wired my particular set of bones and muscles and nervous responses to thrive in the movements and mental focus in the yoga type exercises. The difference is that I am not inviting or meditating on the spirits which have been associated with these movements. I do not practice yoga as the original Hindu religious practice. I am welcoming the Holy Spirit into me and focusing on Jesus Christ. I believe God is able to keep those other spirits away from me. Where the Spirit and presence of God are—those other spirits cannot abide.

If you have wanted to try something like yoga or tai chi, but have concerns, learn what it involves, find out what the Bible says about those things, and pray about it. If you remain uncomfortable, I'd urge you to refrain. If you can allow the physical movements to benefit your body and translate the mindfulness instructions to a focus on prayer and the Holy Spirit, and you feel free in the Lord to participate, I'd say give it a try.

The faith which you have, have as your own conviction before God. Happy is he who does not condemn himself in what he approves. But he who doubts is condemned if he eats, because his eating is not from faith; and whatever is not from faith is sin. Romans 8:22-23

How to start a personal exercise routine

Pick one activity that appeals to you. I'm sure you have an idea of what sounds like a terrible way to exercise, and an idea of what you'd like to try. There's no point in trying something you're sure you'll detest.

You Moms who no longer have a life of your own, there are lots of exercise DVDs you can find for a workout while the kids are napping. Remember that there are many gyms open around the clock these days. And community centers often have child care or exercise classes that show you how you and the kids can get a good workout together! Don't despair that you can't do what you might have once loved to do—just think outside the box and ask around.

Find out what you need to do to get started. I urge you to be sure to get good information, so you can avoid injury and keep motivated when you begin to see results.

Make a plan with realistic goals that are clear and measurable, so you'll know when you've achieved it or not. Lose five pounds. Walk two miles three times a week. You want concrete objectives—not something vague like "lose weight." Break down the big goals into smaller goals. To run a marathon, you'll need to start with being able to make it around the school track without getting winded.

When I started getting serious about my physical fitness, I didn't have a lot of lofty goals. I was 200 pounds at my heaviest, and my starting goal was to make it around the block one time. Then I was happy when I could get by with three meals a day with no snacking between. Easy, little changes, and I was surprised by how the weight started to come off. One goal that cost me a little more nerve was to put on a two-piece bathing suit. I'd never wanted to put on any kind of bathing suit, but one day I met a personal trainer who was competing for a bodybuilding show. So that stuck in my head—the idea of putting on a two-piece bathing suit. And not only did I put on the two-piece, I also entered a bodybuilding competition. And moved on to mini-triathlons, and tactical strength contests. What I'm saying is to have goals. Realistic goals to start, but then move on to the goals that scare you a little.

Check with your doctor to be sure you're in good enough shape to undertake a serious exercise regimen. If you have chronic conditions or have had injuries in the past, make sure you ask a professional about the best way to avoid aggravating your symptoms or re-injuring yourself.

The best way to keep at it when you get tired or bored or busy is to enlist the help of an accountability partner. If all you need is a bunch of gold stars strung one after another on your calendar, go down to the office supply store and buy a packet. If you need someone to call you a 5:00 in the morning to goad your butt out of bed and meet you at the walking trail, find a jogging partner. Personal trainers can help you stay motivated as well as make sure you're going about things the correct way, avoiding injury and meeting your goals.

Plan the new into your weekly calendar. If you see your exercise scheduled, it will incorporate into your day more easily. It won't creep up on you so you're tempted to skip it.

Cut yourself some slack. Don't give up on the whole idea if you miss one day, or even a week. Forgive yourself and keep moving.

Pay attention to your own cues and don't force it if you reach exhaustion or pain or even severe discomfort. These are your body's ways of telling you to back off. Injuring yourself will only discourage you and set you back.

Reminder

Start small. Focus on establishing the habits of activity you want to develop. Small habits will lead to bigger goals every time, if you don't quit.

Make one change at a time. Don't expect to be able to get up an hour earlier, add running to your daily routine, and change your entire diet— all at the same time. Expecting this kind of success is essentially setting yourself up for failure.

Reminder

Don't forget to remember what you like about yourself now. You're not out to change everything about yourself. You're seeking to improve how you feel overall, not become America's next top model.

A final word about exercise

I personally find my daily exercise routine indispensable for feeling good physically as well as for drawing close to God. I work daily to honor God's gift to me by treating my body the best I can. For me, a focus on my body is a proper piece of the puzzle. This may not be the case for you. God wired some people to be their best when they're exercising, and others didn't get this bent. Neither is right or wrong. My whole point is that unless you're on your feet and bending and lifting and squatting all day long, getting intentional whole-body movement into your regular routine can be extremely beneficial.

If you resonate with a focus on physical training and careful eating, there are many paths of wisdom available to serious seekers. Again, I would say, don't let anyone tell you what you must do. No one diet or routine is one-size-fits-all. Your particular body will respond better to this or that type of exercise or nutrition, so find what works for you and care for yourself mindfully.

Also, as with the food you eat, a fantastic physical regimen should not rule you. Self-discipline is a good thing, but when conformity to certain activity standards begins to be most important, it's time to check in with God about what you're really exercising for. Being physically fit won't make you more acceptable to Him.

> *Movement is a medicine for creating change in a*
> *person's physical, emotional, and mental states.*
> *~Carol Welch*

Journal

What would you do if you could do absolutely anything as your regular exercise? Why did you choose this form of activity?

Journal

Take the time to write down ten things you like about yourself as an individual—be it something about your body or about your personality or your approach to life. Copy this list and post it somewhere you can see it several times a day.

Action

In the area of FITNESS, I am going to _____.
I will do _____ by (a specific date) _____.

Prayer

Dear Jesus, I believe You love me, no matter what shape my body is in. Please help me to find the time and energy to exercise and make myself as healthy as I can. Thank you for walking with me every step of the day, whether I am doing it for exercise or just to get my stuff done! This is going to be an adventure! Amen

Check In

My regular exercise consists of
— Bending down to tie my shoes, chasing the dog when he gets out, stretching for the snacks I hid on top of the fridge
— Parking and walking, taking the stairs, using a standing desk, dancing or jogging in place while waiting in lines or cooking.
— A certain number of minutes of deliberate sports for at least 3 times a week.
— Daily workout including stretching, endurance and strength portions.

I've thought about starting an exercise regimen.
— Training for a 5K or starting crossfit has intrigued me.
— Walking in my neighborhood or at the school recreation center would be good.
— I chase kids and run from meeting to meeting all day—I don't need more exercise!
— Walking to the fridge is about as ambitious as I want to be.

My best reason for not starting an exercise regimen is
— I have commitments to my family, my household, and to my job, and there just isn't an hour a day to give to anything else.
— If I just had someone to work out with, I'd love to do it.
— I could start doing something but I'm just not convinced it's really necessary at this point.
— I'm just lazy.

My quality of sleep is
— Great—I wake up feeling pretty rested.
— Kind of rough most nights—I do a lot of tossing and turning.
— I dread going to bed because I don't fall asleep or I wake up a lot. There's no rest.
— Sometimes I sleep fine, sometimes I don't, and I never know why.

6 - FUN: The Wow! Approach

Fun *noun*

1. enjoyment, amusement, or lighthearted pleasure, entertainment, pleasure, recreation, diversion, leisure, relaxation, playful behavior or good humor

2. behavior or an activity that is intended purely for enjoyment

Our daughter Lily brought the "Wow!" approach to life into our family in a big way. When we saw Lily's baby pictures prior to getting to meet her, there was always this little mischievous smile and twinkle in her eye radiating joy. Upon arriving in the States, she did not take life for granted. She would not just walk to the car; she needed to plop down and feel the green grass with her fingers. As we went through town and did our errands, she would gesture and point commenting "Wow!" Wow to the sun, to ice cream, to noisy trucks, to a string of ants on the sidewalk, to the rows of books in the library.

She's gotten used to things now, but the way she looks at things still compels me to appreciate the small things and just enjoy life. Lily's dad and brother are naturally fun people who know how to keep from taking life so seriously, and bringing Lily into the mix has made life even more FUN!

When you get down to it, play is the synthesis of all the topics we've discussed: Faith, Family, Food, and Fitness. Fun can be had doing each one, and more than one at the same time. We worship Jesus and enjoy Christ-centered fellowship with family and friends, find fulfillment in our work, take pleasure in good food with those we love, and we use our bodies to explore the wide world. We enjoy the best life truly has to offer because this is what gets us through the hardest parts.

So I commended pleasure, for there is nothing good for a man under the sun except to eat and to drink and to be merry, and this will stand by him in his toils throughout the days of his life which God has given him under the sun. Ecclesiastes 8:15

Imagine life without games, art, music, sports, jokes, daydreaming, make-believe, spontaneity with friends, pets, getting out in nature, lolly-gagging. When I think about trying to live without the diversions I enjoy so much, my outlook goes dark. The demands of life and work are hard enough—not being able to relax and enjoy life would be intolerable.

Journal

What did you do as a child for fun, for escape? Why don't you do it anymore? What would it take to start doing it again?

The science of fun

More and more studies show that unguided play is necessary for children to learn social skills, express themselves, learn to take risks, and other markers of mental, emotional, and physical development.[20]

School districts that have experimented with reducing outside recess time in favor of more classroom time are discovering increasing rates of disruptive behavior along with decreasing attention spans and academic skills.[21] Neuroscience is constantly coming up with new findings about how healthy brain development depends largely on play.

No one will argue that children need play. But what about the grownups? At what age is it no longer necessary for people to play, relax, stretch, and indulge in fancies? We are driven by to-do lists and paying the bills, and somewhere along the way, play became extravagant and wasteful, a wistful dream from days past.

Good news! The science is coming in around this, too. Big people need play.[22] It is as necessary to living well as good nutrition, sleep, and interpersonal connections.

Play can

- Stimulate imagination and lead to problem solving and adaptation
- Make learning new things easier
- Help you bond and communicate with others
- Boost productivity and job satisfaction
- Get your body moving
- Increase your resilience in hard or tedious situations
- Increase your pleasure in life generally

The experience of pleasurable moments causes the body to release endorphins, which serve to reduce the perception of pain. Endorphins can also boost your immunity, modulate your appetite and improve your overall outlook on life.

Let's laugh! In addition to the flow of endorphins and the suppression of stress hormones, laughing is good for you, too!

Laughter can

- Be a workout for leg, back, stomach, and facial muscles

- Increase tumor-and disease-killing cells in the body
- Lower blood pressure
- Increase oxygen in the blood
- Boost memory, intelligence, and creativity
- Create connection with others[23]

A joyful heart is good medicine, but a broken spirit dries up the bones.
Proverbs 17:22

Journal

List a few ways you can bring fun into you your work day, even while you're going from obligation to obligation, home to work, work to family.

Go play!

Play for adults would be any kind of activity chosen for the pleasure of it, rather than for some reward, like a paycheck. Being in control of the activity is important: making up your own rules and changing the rules when you want. And I'm talking about more than taking a vacation, which more often than not turns out to be more work than play. I mean bring play into every single day.

Play

By this I mean play. As in—play tag with your children. As in jump over the cracks in the sidewalk. Walk your dog in the rain, without an umbrella. Coloring books? Legos? Come on—you know you want to! Go ahead and do things which may look foolish to others. Be merry and enjoy little moments like children do, with great exuberance and joy. Who cares what others think? You're the one who gets to be happy.

Breaks

I know, some days you won't have even fifteen minutes to join the hopscotch game in the neighbor's driveway. But when you find yourself grinding away, step aside for a moment.

A brief break will relax the mental muscle of concentration, so to speak, and let you replenish energy. Often, it can serve to boost your productivity. A bit of interaction with the world out there may work wonders in terms of improving your perspective on what you are laboring over. If nothing more, a quick walk around the block can get your heart rate up and take out the kinks.

My own prescription for health is less paperwork
and more running barefoot through the grass.
~Leslie Grimutter

Hobbies

The list of activities you can take up as a hobby is endless. It can be as simple as painting by number, or as involved as sky-diving or ham radio. It can be something you do by yourself or it can get you out there to engage with other people. You can try different things just to see if you like them, or you can spend hours mastering all the intricacies of a skill few others have.

Just don't let your hobby become work. If you no longer experience joy or that "outside of time" sensation, you're missing the point.

Bucket lists

Do you have a bucket list of things you want to do before you die? Any ideas rattling around in your head, not even committed to paper?

Keeping a list of things you want to do can counteract lethargy and cynicism that can set in when you're working so hard. It gives you another way to be in charge of your life instead of just being along for the ride. Of course, having a list and crossing things off the list once you're done with them are two different things. Don't just build a list. Set some goals, start saving cash and make some reservations.

Journal

Write out your bucket list. If you don't have one, start one. Write down at least three things you want to do before you die. Beside each item, write down one or two things you'd have to accomplish in order to cross off each bucket list item.

Is it fun, truly?

One last thing. If you end up regretting that activity, don't do it. And if someone can wind up hurt in any way, don't do it. You know what I'm talking about. Activities like smoking or drinking may be legal and may have some calming effect, but the truth is that they undermine your body, your mind, and your control of yourself. Don't lend yourself—or anyone else—to harm, or potential harm. This whole book is about building yourself up in the Lord and living an abundant life in a Godly way.

Finally, I guess what I'm saying is to not take life too seriously. Relax, find the little things to enjoy, let the pressure roll off instead of pile up. Have fun things planned to do for when you do get stressed.

Schedule fun time in your calendar and make it happen. Make sure you find time each day for some kind of play. Choose to hang out with people who know how to have the kind of fun you like to have. It is contagious!

Reminder

Everyone has different wiring for fun. What you find fun, I may not. Don't let someone else guilt-trip you into participating in something you don't like and expect to enjoy it. On the other hand, keeping an open mind and trying something you have doubts about may surprise you. Keep an eye out for Wow! Surprises can be good for you!

When we value being cool and in control over granting ourselves the freedom to unleash the passionate, goofy, heartfelt, and soulful expressions of who we are, we betray ourselves. ~Brené Brown

Action

In the area of FUN, I am going to _____.
I will do _____ by (a specific date) _____.

Prayer

Dear Jesus, I believe that You love me no matter how frustrated and uptight I may get. Please help me remember to take time to have fun and be creative! Thank you for putting reminders of Your love and greatness in things big and small all around me. It's a wonderful world filled with fantastic potential! Amen

Check In

I plan down time or fun activities for myself or with others
    — Pretty regularly.
    — When I get desperate for a life outside of work.
    — I don't have time for fun. Life isn't fun.

I'm good at spontaneous fun when I get a whim or when someone invites me along.
    — Yes! I am down for adventures!
    — Spontaneous is kind of hard, but I like to just go do something different every once in a while.
    — No. I have to have it planned ahead.

There is one free-time activity I love to do.
    — Several hours a week.
    — As often as I can, but never enough.
    — I don't really have any regular hobbies, just some things I like to do when I can.
    — No. No hobbies.

(My family and) I have a bucket list of things it would be fun or life-changing to do.
    — Yes! The next one is scheduled.
    — Adventures are easy without planning, so working on a list isn't necessary.
    — There's been some talk about interesting ideas, but no commitment or activity.
    — The idea of a bucket list scares me.

Madison's story

For my mind and body to be in warrior phase and ready to enjoy a vacation, to think of creative ideas at work, and to add value to friend and family relationships, I have to start by being the best version of myself. For me this begins with food and fitness. When I start my day with a balanced breakfast and get to work knowing I have prepared meals and gym clothes with me, it not only puts me in the best mindset, but I can feel the psychological affects and notice the difference in my work quality.

Alternatively, there have been times where I've been off my routine, from setbacks like staying with a friend for the weekend or returning from a long trip. Some fun tends to set me back with my diet, and my body is sensitive to the effects. When I don't plan my meals and have a workout routine, I find myself getting tired by lunch and napping at the end of the day.

I think there's a balance between fitness, food and fun, and I'm the happiest when I incorporate all three. For me this looks like planning that vacation but packing healthy snacks, immediately going to the grocery store upon arrival, and only eating out once per day. Some people disagree with this because a vacation is supposed to be a time when you "relax," but personally I need to feel healthy and energized to fully relax.

82

7 - Are You Going To Make It?

My precious, strong, and brave woman trying to hold your little corner of the world together, if you realize that you are in trouble beyond what you can fix yourself, everything I've said still applies. I'll add a few ideas to help you start the work of restoring from burnout and all your wounds.

First of all, turn to Jesus. Without Jesus, everything else I've said is just more to do, more to accomplish. You may reap some benefits, but the core of your recovery is inside, in your thoughts and attitude and where you receive your value from. If you are secure in Jesus' love for you, two things are true:

1. Nothing else matters. It's true. God loves you completely and deeply, and even if you never accomplish anything for the rest of your life, nothing will change that. You belong to Him.

But when the kindness of God our Savior and His love for mankind appeared, He saved us, not on the basis of deeds which we have done in righteousness, but according to His mercy. Titus 3:4-5

2. Everything else is easier. Yes, Jesus is enough—nothing changes this—but having this reality as the foundation makes all your efforts easier. You have God's wisdom when you need it, and you have the encouragement and support of fellow Christians when you ask for it. You have the power of the Holy Spirit to strengthen you. You no longer have to figure it out by yourself.

For it is God who is at work in you, both to will and to work for His good pleasure. Philippians 2:13

Trust in the Lord with all your heart and do not lean on your own understanding. In all your ways acknowledge Him, and He will make your paths straight. Proverbs 3:5-6

After you've made things right with Jesus, seek professional help. Sometimes coming back from tough stuff is simply beyond what we can pull together ourselves. One thing the Bible tells us is to seek wise counsel. Choose a Christian counselor who will steer you toward insights or conclusions that are in agreement with your faith.

The beginning of wisdom is: Acquire wisdom; and with all your acquiring, get understanding. Proverbs 4:7

The way of a fool is right in his own eyes, but a wise man is he who listens to counsel. Proverbs 12:15

Finally
The thief comes only to steal and kill and destroy; I came that they may have life, and have it abundantly. John 10:10

'For I know the plans that I have for you,' declares the Lord, 'plans for welfare and not for calamity to give you a future and a hope.' Jeremiah 29:11

Dear woman, I pray for you! I pray that you can grasp what I have learned and develop an amazing and effective warrior woman's life. My own life used to be based on performance and addictive behaviors, even while I was helping others find their way. God got my attention by finally getting me to see that I was building on a sandy shore instead of a solid rock foundation. He led me on a long journey of learning to let Him fill that desperate ache and numb void inside that nothing at all could touch. Now, it is a profoundly intimate relationship with Jesus that has freed me from addiction and co-dependency to a completely different life. This is what I want for you—an unbelievable experience of the power of the Holy Spirit of God to radically transform your life right before your eyes.

To that end, I've given you my best wisdom. I hope and pray that you will find your way from wounded to warrior woman through Faith, Family, Food, Fitness and Fun!

Reminder

Give yourself time. It just takes time. Enjoy the journey and the good moments along the way; don't despise being in process. None of us ever arrives on this side anyway.

Reminder

Take baby steps. Yes, it may be a big mess when you step back and look at it, but the truth is that you can't fix it all right now. Try only one new thing at a time. Plot out the small baby steps you need to try and stay after them.

Reminder

Learn your own signals that you're reaching a stress level. For instance, when you realize that you've been waffling over the simplest decisions, or when you're angry for no reason, do a quick self-check. Try a HALT check (Hungry-Angry-Lonely-Tired) for good signals that you need to practice some self-care as soon as possible. Pay attention these next few months and you can probably begin to identify your own unique cues.

Ladies, pay attention to your monthly signals so that hormone-driven mood swings and fatigue don't overwhelm you unawares. You don't have to be ruled by your menstrual cycle, so when you become aware that it might be about that time, cut yourself some extra slack, don't take things so seriously, and practice responding in ways that lead to peace instead of more stress.

Reminder

Do not be too proud to ask for help. If you're in crisis, a safe outlet right now is critical. Counseling is not permanent—it's to help you find safety and safe footing in a crisis.

9 - Abundant Life

Here we are at the end of the book! You've done some reading and self-examination and prayer. How do you feel? Are you convinced that you can stop being the walking wounded and become a warrior woman in the Lord?

One thing that surprises me at different points in this journey is that sometimes I catch myself feeling a little guilty at how well things are going. Sometimes the little voice that said I didn't matter and I wasn't worthy will try to dig at me with the idea that I don't deserve all that hard work to have paid off. That I don't deserve the amazing experience of being married to my best friend, or to have good relationships with my two great kids, or to have a body that's both normal weight and extremely healthy.

When I think about it, there are other bits of icing on the cake. Some of those folks who weren't supportive at the start of our adoption journey have come alongside us in amazing ways, like helping to pay some of the therapy bills. I've found myself meeting regularly with a group of totally cool women. They're amazing and real about life and we hold each other up in accountability and prayer, not just in nice sounding platitudes with no substance behind it. So, God showed up. The people and the resources showed up, too, the ones God had in mind to help me along when I really opened my heart to receive all the goodness out there, not just dwell on the hard and awful parts.

That "I don't deserve it" thing is a lie I have to be careful to not give space to. I have what I have because God really did bring me to that abundant life that He promised. God did show up, and brought me from wounded to warrior.

It is my prayer that you feel hopeful and excited! You know how hard life can be, but I hope you have eyes wide open about how good it can be. I hope you're convinced that you really do have access to effective tools to help you not just manage, but create an abundant life—you and Jesus!

As if I haven't said enough already, I want to share two concepts that can help you stay interested in finding and keeping a healthy balance in all the areas of your life: giving yourself permission and course corrections.

Give yourself permission

If you haven't yet, give yourself permission. I mean give yourself permission to admit that you are feeling overwhelmed. If you don't own up that you're struggling, all the good ideas in the world are just ideas.

Give yourself permission to be wounded and imperfect, to need help and not have all the answers. That's the case anyway. Nobody on earth is whole. Only Jesus has all the answers.

When you need to, forgive yourself for letting yourself down, letting others down, letting God down. Then keep moving. Don't continue to beat yourself up. Nagging guilt comes from the devil, but God's forgiveness is complete, and so should yours be. Circling back around to be hard on yourself yields no benefit, but it will make your efforts harder.

Give yourself permission to try something, but also to give it up if it's really not you. I don't mean permission to quit when it gets hard. I mean if you've been running for six months and you've hated every minute of it, don't run. Take up ballroom dancing or snowshoeing or something that you don't hate. If you've tried vegan and you're weak all the time, get some animal protein into your diet.

Except for the only way to begin a relationship with Jesus, there's no such thing as a one-size-fits-all solution. When you discover the unique ways He made you, you can begin to love yourself and love taking the best care of yourself. If it doesn't work for you, it's probably not honoring God to stubbornly pursue it.

Journal

What do you need to give yourself permission to do, dear one? Write down a couple ways you know you can give yourself a break. Write down why it's hard to give yourself permission to do something different, then write down a different way to think about it.

Course corrections

When a plane takes off, the pilot will set a direction, and she has to check in periodically to see if the plane is still heading in the right direction. If not, she'll make course corrections. The reason is that, while one degree off for a few miles won't take you very far off course, one degree off over enough miles could take you to New York City instead of Atlanta.

When you're working your goals and implementing what you feel will bring balance back into your life, you may at some point discover that you're not heading where you intended. For instance, you joined a Sunday School class to get more into the Word, but now you're on the leadership team and planning events every month, which is just adding to your overwhelm all the more. Give yourself permission to course correct and get yourself off leadership. (They'll survive without you!) If you've been jogging three miles three times a week, but you're getting more physical pain than relief from it, try walking, or cutting it to two miles. You don't have to scrub it all and start over. Just make a simple change. Course correction.

You'll be course correcting for the rest of your life. It was a huge relief when I realized this simple thing. Now course correcting and giving myself permission have been two of the best tools in my toolbox.

Journal

What small course corrections might you start implementing in your life? List a couple things you're struggling with and a few things you might try a bit differently, to see if it will work better.

Final Check In

I read the whole book and worked through the assessment and response journaling questions.
- — Yes! I finished it all.
- — Started off well but didn't quite make it.
- — I didn't have time to write things out but I read it all and thought about it here and there--does that count?

My three main signals that I'm approaching overload and need to get back to center are
1. _____
2. _____
3. _____

The three biggest takeaways that came to me are
1. _____
2. _____
3. _____

The three things I am going to start working on are
1. _____
2. _____
3. _____

Three immediate goals I have—with dates!—are
1. _____
2. _____
3. _____

The one thing that concerns me the most about all of this is
_____.

There's only one way to be saved

Reality in a few simple sentences…

For the wages of sin is death, but the free gift of God is eternal life in Christ Jesus our Lord. Romans 6:23

For God so loved the world, that He gave His only begotten Son, that whoever believes in Him shall not perish, but have eternal life. John 3:16

- God created us, loves us, and wants fellowship with us, but our sins separate us from God, who is perfect and holy.

- The penalty for our sins is death and eternal separation from God.

- Jesus Christ died on the cross in our place and rose again.

- If you trust that God accepts Jesus' death on the cross on your behalf, instead of any good works you can do, you are right with God and have eternal life with Him.

Do you acknowledge that you need to deal with your sins to get right with God?

A prayer you can pray

Dear God, I believe that You love me and want a relationship with me. I know that my sins separate me from you and I turn my back on sin. I accept that Jesus died on the cross in my place, and I receive the forgiveness you extend to me. I thank you for the promise of eternal life and I ask you to help me by the Holy Spirit to live the right way every day. Thank you! Amen

That's it! Now you have everything you need to live an abundant and victorious life! Remember, you may have some hard work to do and some things to straighten out, but now Jesus is with you and, I promise, you really do have all you need.

Kris' sample meal plan

Here is a sample of a basic meal plan I use for overall health on a daily basis. I rotate through variations on a regular basis, since variety is important for a few reasons. Try different things to discover what works for your portability needs and nutrition needs. Also, since everyone's schedule is different, your meal schedule will probably vary from mine. Generally speaking, it is good for the body to eat every 3 to 4 hours.

My blender is a portable shaker bottle or electric countertop type, depending on where I'm prepping. I carry a cold pack if I will be needing to prep something away from the house or when I'm traveling. This may be more trouble than you want to undertake, but for me it's worth the effort to not deal with sugar swings and hunger. Again, it depends on your body and what works best.

Meal 1 - 4:45 am Heading to gym
One scoop of protein powder (20 grams), one scoop of green powder, and one scoop of red powder from Trader Joe's. I mix everything with a handful of ice in the blender at home and carry this to the gym.

My water jug In addition, I will bring a gallon of water (prepared the night before) mixed with 1 teaspoon each lemon juice, Bragg's Amino

Acids, Bragg's Apple Cider Vinegar, and mineral drops. In order to consume all the things I add daily, I have to drink the whole gallon throughout the day. I enjoy the taste and the health benefits!

If this is overwhelming and seems more like a chore, one gallon of spring water daily is fine. Remember to keep it simple. It's a personal preference based on your lifestyle.

Meal 2 - 8:30 am
4 oz. protein, ¼ cup of grain, and one fat

Lately, I have been following more of a Paleo kind of meal plan and my breakfast will look something along these lines: 4 oz. cooked ground turkey with ¼ c of tomato sauce, ½ avocado, 5 oz. of sweet potato mixed with cinnamon. For another fat alternative, you can use 1 tbsp. coconut oil on the sweet potato instead of the avocado.

Waffles (one serving recipe)
3 egg whites, one whole egg
¼ cup of grain (oatmeal, oat bran, cream of rice, grits-choose one grain)
5 oz. of your favorite fruit (blueberries, strawberries, banana-choose one fruit),
1 tbsp. of cinnamon, pinch of baking powder
one packet of sweetener if you use sweetener. (I don't use any kind of sweetener since I avoid sugar.)
Mix the batter into a waffle iron, or use a pie pan, or muffin pan at 375 for 15 minutes. Make sure you use non-stick spray for your pan. When your waffle is cooled off, wrap with aluminum foil and place in your freezer. I like to wrap them as single servings since I will usually multiply this recipe and bake 5 to 7 in one batch. These waffles keep and travel well.

Meal 3 - Noon
4 oz. protein, 1 fat, 2 cups of veggies cooked or uncooked, one grain (optional)

If I am eating grain, I will do fried rice.

Fried Rice

Preheat skillet with non-stick spray and sauté ½ cup of onions. When onions are cooked, add one whole egg. (The yellow yoke is your fat). Mix it all together. Next, add in ½ cup of cooked brown rice and 1 ½ cups of your favorite raw veggies. I like to use mushrooms and graded/riced broccoli. Mix together and add in 4 oz. of your favorite protein. I use chopped cooked chicken breast. I will add 2 tbsp. of "Bragg Liquid Aminos" which is a natural soy sauce alternative. If you don't have wheat or alcohol allergies, soy sauce is a great all-purpose seasoning. The fried rice carries very well and is easy to store.

Salad

2 cups of raw veggies of your choice (I use spinach, broccoli slaw, and sprouts.
1 tbs flax seed, 1 tsp chia seeds, 1 tsp rice vinegar, 1 tsp of balsamic vinegar (no sugar) and ½ avocado.
4 oz of your favorite protein (optional). I like to add chicken.
Squirt a dash of lemon or lime juice on top of the salad.

Meal 4 - 3:30 pm

In order to avoid overeating at dinner, I will eat a snack. The key is to make this easy to carry along and eat on the go.

Snack options
- Ready-made protein shake. If I am near in outlet, I will use my portable blender for a shake. If I need energy, I will put one scoop of green tea powder into the shake or some kind of green powder.
- One piece of fruit and a handful of nuts. (I don't use nuts since nuts cause cravings for me and can be addictive.)
- One portion of Greek yogurt
- Protein bar (Make sure you find one that is low in sugar and carbs-clean eating.)
- Handful of carrots or celery with one serving of guacamole or hummus
- One hardboiled egg
- 2 slices of turkey with or without a piece of fruit

- When we were in China, I used 20 grams of Paleo beef/turkey jerky.
- Green drink or smoothie (Watch out for high sugar content since this can raise your blood sugar)

Smoothie
½ cup of frozen blueberries
1 cup of milk (almond, soy, coconut, or low-fat milk) (I like to get Horizon's milk with Omega added to it.)
1 tbsp. of cinnamon (optional)
Mix everything together in portable blender bottle or electric blender.

Meal 5 - 6 pm
4 oz. protein, 2 cups of veggies, optional fat and optional starch.

These are some of our favorite dinner recipes.

Pizza
2 cups of riced cauliflower OR 2 cups of shredded zucchini (I use the food processor, but you can buy ready-riced/shredded at most grocery stores in produce section.)
Add 5 egg whites and one whole egg mixed together in mixing bowl.
Pour this batter into a non-stick sprayed pan of your choice. I use a round pizza pan but a cookie sheet will work also.
Cook crust at 350 degrees for 10 minutes or until crust is solid.
One cup of sugar-free pizza sauce onto crust. Top with any other veggies of your choice.
Cook for 10 to 15 minutes more.
Note: If you don't like the zucchini or riced cauliflower, you can use ½ cup cooked brown rice as the crust.

Vegetable Spaghetti
2 cups of grated veggies of your choice. You can buy veggies that are grated or cut like noodles in your produce section.
Place veggies in a pan. You can add fat by adding one tbsp. coconut oil or just use your non-stick spray. Add one tsp of the following to veggies while cooking: fresh garlic, ginger, and turmeric, a dash of cayenne pepper to taste.

Add in 4 oz. of cooked ground turkey or beef. I always use ground turkey. After you add your meat, add ½ cup of sugar-free tomato sauce and mix it all together. When food is plated, add ½ cup of avocado on top of pasta. If you don't like avocado, try cooking with one tbsp. of coconut oil or olive oil.

Slow Cooker Tacos
Place one package of ground turkey with one package of taco seasoning into a crock pot. In addition, add one sliced onion and one sliced green or red pepper (into the crock pot). I usually cook for 6 to 8 hours on low if I am away from house and I crumble and break up the meat when I get home if it went into the crock pot frozen.

I will have side dishes to serve on table during dinner of the following: shredded lettuce, sliced avocados, salsa, sour cream, and black beans. Corn shells, tortillas, or large lettuce leaves as shell.
This is a great family dish to make for dinner. Leftovers store real well for lunch the following day.

Meal 6 - Bedtime
Optional Snacks - choose one
- 6 cups of cooked popcorn. (no salt-I use an air popper)
- 1 cup of Greek yogurt plain, non-fat mixed with 6 oz. fruit
- 5 egg whites with one whole egg, scrambled

"Sweets"
Mousse recipe
One cup of organic fat-free milk mixed for 2 minutes in a food processor. Add both 5 oz. frozen fruit of your choice and one scoop of protein powder. Although the protein is optional—I like the additional protein. Mix on high with food processor for 3 minutes. This whips up like a mousse and is delicious. Make sure you are not lactose intolerant.

Apple cobbler recipe
Heat pan on medium and non-stick spray the pan. Mince a whole apple into little pieces and cook apples on hot pan until golden brown. When golden brown, add one tbsp of cinnamon or pumpkin pie spice. Add one cup of non-fat Greek yogurt on top. Eat while hot.

On-the-go options, including overseas traveling

- Turkey, beef, bison jerky-single packs are great for portion control.
- Salmon, chicken, or tuna in cans or packs. Make sure you get the kind the kind that do not need a can opener. Also, any other kind of protein that do not require refrigeration
- Mustard and salsa or any kind of condiment-avoid any kind of condiments in glass since you don't want anything breaking in your luggage! I am not particularly fond of dry tuna and like to use the mustard or salsa as a way to moisten the tuna.
- Single packages of protein powder. You can also measure them ahead of time and put one scoop of powder (depending on serving size) into a small zip lock bag. They store very well in luggage.
- Single serving bags of any kinds of nuts. Almonds are a great choice. Be careful of a lot of salt.
- Single serving sizes of peanut butter. If any kinds of nuts or peanut butter are addictive- avoid. Check for added sugar.
- I don't eat nuts so for fats, I get single serving sizes of coconut oil from Trader Joe's and will use the single servings as my fats.
- Rice cakes are a great carry on for travel as well. You can get unsalted brown rice cakes as well for more of a complex carb kind of starch.
- If you are carrying an ice pack you can get single packs of guacamole found in the produce section of stores
- Unsweetened applesauce or plastic containers of fruit. This is not the healthiest choice in terms of depleting all the nutrients compared to fresh fruit but it is an option. Stick to fruits that are easy to open and won't make too much mess.
- Protein bars. I find protein bars addictive and more like candy bars, but if protein bars work for your body and don't set you up craving, there are some great protein bar choices.
- Single serving size of mini carrots, celery, and any other veggies that are easy to open, if you have some kind of ice pack. I like to use the plastic bag of beets in the produce section but you have to be careful opening the bag since you don't want purple juice from the beets all over you. (Pack kids' scissors to

help with opening!) Veggies are such a great option. Single serve packs are sometimes hard to find, but you can always prepare ahead of time by portioning servings into single bags. I like to use green beans or sugar snap peas in zip lock bags. Again, this might not be the tastiest however, if you use the mini serving of guacamole for dipping it works! Also, bring some sea salt with you to help with the taste.

- Those waffles travel well and don't need an icepack of you're going to eat them the day you pack them.

About Kris

Dr. Kristen Nugent has taught Social Work and maintained a private practice for 20 years, specializing in work with individuals and family around such issues as addiction, co-dependency, family of origin trauma, eating disorders and wellness. Passionate about helping people lead their best lives, she also leads workshops in the area of wellness and addiction. Dr. Nugent mostly appreciates spending time with her husband and their two children. The Nugents have recently transplanted to Texas. You can find out more about what Dr. Nugent has to offer at her website krisnugenthealthylifestyle.com.

References

1. Bonelli, R., Dew, R. E., Koenig, H. G., Rosmarin, D. H., Vasegh. S. (2012). Religious and Spiritual Factors in Depression: Review and Integration of the Research. *Hindawi.* Retrieved from https://www.hindawi.com/journals/drt/2012/962860/
2. Social and Humanitarian Assistance - The family—society's building block (bullet points, n.d.). *Nations Encyclopedia.* Retrieved from https://www.nationsencyclopedia.com/United-Nations/Social-and-Humanitarian-Assistance-THE-FAMILY-SOCIETY-S-BUILDING-BLOCK.html
3. Harvard Women's Health Watch (December 2013). Stress and your heart. *Harvard Health Publishing.* Retrieved from https://www.health.harvard.edu/heart-health/stress-and-your-heart
4. Hansen, F. (December 2017). How does stress affect your immune system? *The Adrenal Fatigue Solution.* Retrieved from https://adrenalfatiguesolution.com/stress-immune-system/
5. Press release. (2013). Stress and sleep. *American Psychological Association.* Retrieved from https://www.apa.org/news/press/releases/stress/2013/sleep

6. Scheiner, G. (August 2016). How Stress hormones raise blood sugar. *Insulin Nation.* Retrieved from https://insulinnation.com/treatment/how-stress-hormones-raise-blood-sugar/

7. 4 Ways stress impacts digestion. (2018) *Institute for the Psychology of Eating* Retrieved from https://psychologyofeating.com/4-ways-stress-impacts-digestion/

8. Petrangelo A., and Watson, S. (June 2017). The effects of stress on your body. *Healthline.* Retrieved from https://www.healthline.com/health/stress/effects-on-body

9. Freishtat, A. (July 2012). The stress-exercise connection: how does this work? *Orthodox Union.* Retrieved from https://www.ou.org/life/health/the-stress-exercise-connection-how-does-this-work/

10. Willett, W. C. (2019). How stress can make us overeat. *Harvard Health Publishing.* Retrieved from https://www.health.harvard.edu/healthbeat/how-stress-can-make-us-overeat

11. Singh, S. (February 2015). Critical reasons for crashes investigated in the National Motor Vehicle Crash Causation Survey. (Traffic Safety Facts Crash•Stats. Report No. DOT HS 812 115). *National Highway Traffic Safety Administration.* Retrieved from https://crashstats.nhtsa.dot.gov/Api/Public/ViewPublication/812115

12. Bjarnadottir, A. (May 2019). 7 Nutrient deficiencies that are incredibly common. *Healthline.* Retrieved from https://www.healthline.com/nutrition/7-common-nutrient-deficiencies

13. Moody, L. (n.d.). These 8 foods are wreaking havoc on your hormones. *mindbodygreen.* Retrieved from https://www.mindbodygreen.com/0-29200/these-8-foods-are-wreaking-havoc-on-your-hormones.html

14. Leech, J. (July 2019). What are trans fats, and are they bad for you? *Healthline.* Retrieved from https://www.healthline.com/nutrition/why-trans-fats-are-bad

15. Ruddock, V. (2019). Dangers of food additives and preservatives. *LoveToKnow.* Retrieved from https://greenliving.lovetoknow.com/dangers-food-additives-preservatives

16. Price, A. (January 2016). Metabolic syndrome: proven diet and natural treatment plan. *Dr Axe.* Retrieved from https://draxe.com/health/heart-health/metabolic-syndrome/
17. Infographic. (2017). Artificial sweeteners and toxic side effects. *Dr. Osborne.* Retrieved from https://drpeterosborne.com/artificial-sweeteners-toxic-side-effects/
18. Mawer, R. (October 2016). 6 Reasons why high-fructose corn syrup is bad for you. *Healthline.* Retrieved from https://www.healthline.com/nutrition/why-high-fructose-corn-syrup-is-bad
19. Harmful effects of diet pills and supplements. (October 2018). *Futures Recovery Healthcare.* Retrieved from https://futuresrecoveryhealthcare.com/knowledge-center/harmful-effects-diet-pills-supplements/
20. Barker, J. E., Semenov, A. D., Michaelson, L., Provan, L. S., Snyder, H. R., Munakata, Y. (June 2014). Less-structured time in children's daily livedpredicts self-directed executive functioning. *Frontiers in Psychology.* Retrieved from https://www.ncbi.nlm.nih.gov/pmc/articles/PMC4060299/
21. Flannery, M. E. (July 2016). After years of cuts to playtime, parents and educators are bringing recess back. *NEA Today.* Retrieved from http://neatoday.org/2016/07/14/bringing-recess-back/

22. Wallace, J. (May 2017). Why it's good for grown-ups to go play. *The Washington Post.* Retrieved from https://www.washingtonpost.com/national/health-science/why-its-good-for-grown-ups-to-go-play/2017/05/19/99810292-fd1f-11e6-8ebe-6e0dbe4f2bca_story.html?noredirect=on
23. Nagdeve, M. (May 2019). 10 Impressive benefits of laughter. *Organic Facts.* Retrieved from https://www.organicfacts.net/health-benefits/other/health-benefits-of-laughter.html

www.ingramcontent.com/pod-product-compliance
Lightning Source LLC
Chambersburg PA
CBHW031323040426
42443CB00005B/196